Synthesis Lectures on Computer Science

The series publishes short books on general computer science topics that will appeal to advanced students, researchers, and practitioners in a variety of areas within computer science.

Jungyeul Park

Evaluation by Alignment

A Framework for Robust End-to-End NLP Assessment

Springer

Jungyeul Park
Culture Technology Institute
Korea Advanced Institute of Science
and Technology (KAIST)
Daejeon, Korea (Republic of)

ISSN 1932-1228 ISSN 1932-1686 (electronic)
Synthesis Lectures on Computer Science
ISBN 978-3-032-16562-6 ISBN 978-3-032-16563-3 (eBook)
https://doi.org/10.1007/978-3-032-16563-3

This Springer imprint is published by the registered company Springer Nature Switzerland AG
The registered company address is: Gewerbestrasse 11, 6330 Cham, Switzerland

To Emma and Daniel

Foreword

In 1998, I received an application for a master's program from a brilliant Korean student who had completed his undergraduate work in computer science in Korea. He had achieved promising results in language-processing projects and was eager to combine computer science with linguistic knowledge. We were delighted to welcome him to our university in Paris. Since then, Jungyeul Park has become a prolific researcher in natural language processing (NLP) and taught across North America, Europe, and Korea.

In this book, Jungyeul Park addresses a persistent flaw that affects standard evaluation procedures used in developing NLP applications, and proposes a new generation of evaluation systems.

High-quality evaluation is essential to the development and improvement of NLP systems. It enables researchers not only to select the most effective technologies but also to guide their evolution.

Ideally, evaluation procedures should be applicable to systems employing any underlying technology and should allow comparisons independent of internal operation or implementation choices. This implies that they should remain ahead of cutting-edge approaches to enable fair and meaningful comparisons with the state of the art.

In practice, however, this has rarely been the case. Available evaluation metrics have typically been fully compatible only with already established technologies. Meanwhile, researchers have developed NLP systems that process an increasingly diverse range of languages, explored new methods of segmenting text into words, morphemes, phrases and sentences, and experimented with various neural architectures. Training data now follow different annotation conventions. Practices have gradually diverged from reference resources which still serve as benchmarks for evaluation, such as the Penn Treebank. The differences—steps in methods and data representation—are not relevant to system evaluation. Yet the metrics most commonly used today—accuracy, F-measure, BLEU, ROUGE, GLEU, chrF, LAS/UAS, EVALB and others—are no longer well suited to the diversity that characterizes modern NLP. Newer metrics that rely on large language models

(LLMs) or on geometry within high-dimensional embedding spaces have been proposed, but their reliability is uncertain, and they are not widely adopted.

To address the need for comparing systems that use diverse linguistic representations, Park designed and tested more flexible evaluation techniques. His approach establishes structured correspondences between linguistic representations, leveraging alignment technologies to refine standard metrics and make them compatible with today's diversity in NLP.

This book will be invaluable to researchers and innovators who seek reliable, accurate, unbiased methods for assessing NLP systems and improving their performance.

Paris, France
November 2025

Eric G. C. Laporte

Preface

The idea behind this book took shape gradually, through teaching and research that often intertwined more closely than I had anticipated. The first prototype of what would eventually become the JP-series algorithms examined in this book originated in the preprocessing component I designed for *LING 242: Computational Tools for Linguistic Analysis*, a course I taught at the University of British Columbia between 2021 and 2025. The prefix "JP" stands for *jointly preprocessing*, referring to the alignment based approach that links sentence and word boundaries as a preprocessing step before actual evaluation begins. What started as a teaching exercise, aimed at helping students understand how raw text becomes analyzable linguistic data, eventually evolved into a broader research agenda on how such processes could be evaluated in a principled and reproducible way.

In most areas of natural language processing, standard evaluation tools have long been established—F_1 scores for parsing, BLEU for machine translation, and ERRANT-based measures for grammatical error correction. Yet, for text preprocessing—sentence boundary detection, tokenization, normalization—there remained no comparable framework for consistent assessment. What seemed a simple task at first soon revealed itself as a surprisingly intricate problem. Differences between gold standard and system outputs often arose not from errors in content but from misaligned boundaries, making evaluation both technically and conceptually challenging.

With the support of dedicated research assistants and generous funding from the *Students as Partners* initiative at UBC and the *Academy of Korean Studies*, we began developing what we called JP- PREPROCESSING, followed by JP- EVALB and JP- ERRANT. The guiding principle was straightforward yet ambitious: to extend alignment-based evaluation, which has been widely used in machine translation, to a broad range of NLP tasks including preprocessing, constituency parsing, and grammatical error correction.

Over time, this framework developed into what I now-call **Evaluation by Alignment**, a unified approach to assessing linguistic structure and behavior across the full end-to-end pipeline of language processing. The underlying methods and results have been presented at the *International Conference on Computational Linguistics*, the *Annual Conference of the*

North American Chapter of the Association for Computational Linguistics, and published in *Computational Linguistics*. This volume brings them together for the first time within a coherent theoretical and methodological framework.

In preparing this manuscript, I have used large language models for paraphrasing, grammatical and consistency checks, and proofreading.

I hope this book serves both researchers and practitioners who seek not only to build language technologies but also to understand how to evaluate them fairly and rigorously. Behind every algorithm presented here lies a simple motivation: to make evaluation as transparent and reproducible as the models it measures.

Daejeon, South Korea
October 2025

Jungyeul Park

Acknowledgments This book reflects not only my own work but also the efforts, generosity, and companionship of many people who have accompanied me on this long journey. I owe them more than I can express here.

I would like to express my sincere gratitude to *Prof. Eric Laporte*, whose insight and encouragement have accompanied this project from its early stages. I am deeply grateful that he agreed to write the Foreword to this book.

I would like to thank *Eunkyul Leah Jo* and *Junrui Wang*, who worked with me as research assistants and helped me implement every component of the JP- ALGORITHM with care, patience, and creativity. Their contributions turned ideas into real systems.

I am deeply grateful to the undergraduate and MDS-CL capstone students at UBC who contributed to the development of JP- PREPROCESSING and JP- EVALB, from implementation to experimentation: *Angela Yoonseo Park*, *Grace Tianjiao Zhang*, *Izia Xiaoxiao Wang*, and *Mingjia Mao*. Their curiosity and persistence laid the foundation for this project.

My sincere thanks go to my colleagues and friends at *Open Writing Evaluation*, who shared the long journey of designing grammatical error correction systems and their evaluation methods: *Mengyang Qiu*, *Yang Gu*, *Zihao Huang*, *Tran Minh Nguyen*, *Chris Qingyu Gao*, and *Celine Siliang Liu*. Their collaboration gave the JP-framework both breadth and depth, particularly in the development of JP- ERRANT.

Over the years, many students have worked with me on a wide range of research projects, including *Yige Chen*, *Jae Ihn*, *Min Zeng*, *Jessie Jiexin Kuang*, *John Yuxi Wang*, *Agatha Ai Ka Lee*, *Cheyanne Hui Yin Lim*, *Lusha Wang*, *Yuchen Li*, *Shawn Yi Song*, and *Su Yuan*. I am especially indebted to two colleagues who have collaborated with me for almost a decade on learner corpus research, *Jayoung Song* and *KyungTae Lim*.

I would like to express my appreciation to my colleagues at the University of British Columbia—*Miikka Silfverberg*, *Garrett Nicolai*, and *Jian Zhu*—as well as my teaching assistants *Yadong Liu*, *Changbing Yang*, *Edith Coates*, *Anna Stacey*, *Mingcong Li*, and *Sara Mirjalili*, for their support, discussions, and friendship during my years of teaching and research.

To all the MDS-CL students at UBC who have since become cherished friends—*Zhiyi*, *Xihan*, *Berhrooz*, *Jacob Jae hyeuk*, *Biya*, *Gordon*, *Dave*, *Sherry*, *Grace*, *Ziggy*, *Yue*, *Christy*, *Hao Chen*, *Minsi*, *Trang*, *Cindy*, *Nicole*, *Jiao*, *David*, and *Jonathan*—thank you for brightening both my academic and personal life with your warmth, humor, and friendship.

To all undergraduate students who enrolled in LING242 and helped test the JP-ALGORITHMS, and to those who later joined my team to pursue related research projects—*Eitan*, *Vivaan*, *Aryan*, *Ankur*, *Benjamin*, *Danny*, *Buyang*, *Emily*, *Nicholas*, *Casey*, and *Kevin*—thank you for your enthusiasm, insight, and willingness to experiment with ideas still in formation. Your questions often revealed what I had overlooked, and your curiosity continually reminded me why teaching and research belong together.

My other side of UBC life was made special by my friends at the School of Music, especially all the trumpet players with whom I performed in more than ten concerts between 2022 and 2024: *Azeen*, *Lamby*, *Bryce*, *Andy*, *Finn*, *Ben*, *Silas*, *Marcus*, *Haruka*, *Isabella*, and *Kendra*. Their patience with me as a non-professional trumpet player, and their friendship, made countless rehearsals and every concert a joy.

My heartfelt thanks extend to my close friends in Vancouver who made daily life brighter: *Yundong*, *Alice*, and *Celine*, and their partners *Kiki*, *Mike*, and *Ben*. Their dinners, laughter, and warmth made every week feel like home.

Finally, my deepest gratitude goes to my family for their unconditional love and support—wherever I may be in France, the United States, Canada, or Korea, as has often been the case over the past twenty-five years. They have been the quiet strength behind every page of this book.

This book was based upon work partially supported by the *Students as Partners* Initiative at The University of British Columbia, which contributed to the development of Chap. 3, and by the *2024 Korean Studies Grant Program* of the Academy of Korean Studies (AKS-2024-R-094), which provided support for the development of Chaps. 4 and 5.

The writing and completion of the book as a whole were further supported by the Institute of Information & Communications Technology Planning & Evaluation (IITP) grant funded by the Korea government (Ministry of Science and ICT; MSIT) (No.~RS-2025-25441313, *Professional AI Talent Development Program for Multimodal AI Agents*).

Competing Interests The author has no competing interests to declare that are relevant to the content of this manuscript.

Ethics Approval This book is theoretical in nature and does not involve studies with human participants or animals; therefore, ethics approval was not required.

Contents

Acronyms

BEA	Building Educational Applications
BIO	Beginning–inside–outside
CEFR	Common European Framework of Reference
FN	False negative
FP	False positive
GEC	Grammatical error correction
HOO	Helping Our Own
LAS	Labeled attachment score
MT	Machine translation
NER	Named entity recognition
NLP	Natural language processing
POS	Part-of-speech
PTB	Penn Treebank
SBD	Sentence boundary detection *or* sentence boundary disambiguation
SRL	Semantic role labeling
TED	Tree edit distance
TP	True positive
UAS	Unlabeled attachment score
W&I corpus	Write and Improve corpus

1 Introduction

1.1 The Role of Evaluation in NLP

Evaluation is the foundation of **natural language processing** (NLP), providing the means by which systems are compared, progress is measured, and the very notion of improvement is defined. Every milestone in NLP, whether in parsing, tagging, translation, or generation, has been achieved and recognized through evaluation. Without reliable metrics, it would be impossible to assess whether a new model truly advances the state of the art or merely differs in implementation.

Historically, evaluation in NLP emerged from the paradigm of modular architectures, where systems were decomposed into clearly defined components such as tokenizers, part-of-speech (POS) taggers, parsers, and generators. Each module was evaluated independently using task-specific benchmarks and well-defined gold standards. Accuracy, F-score, and related measures provided simple, interpretable numbers that reflected system performance under controlled conditions. The modular nature of early NLP made such metrics effective: each task had a single, unambiguous output format and a canonical notion of correctness.

However, as NLP evolved toward integrated, end-to-end systems spanning from raw text input to complex linguistic or semantic outputs, the premises that once ensured fair comparison began to erode. End-to-end neural models no longer rely on shared preprocessing pipelines or standardized segmentation; instead, they operate directly on character or subword sequences, often producing outputs that differ in form but not in meaning. In such cases, evaluation frameworks that depend on exact matching between system output and gold annotation can fail to capture genuine linguistic equivalence. A system that tokenizes differently, generates alternative phrasing, or outputs valid paraphrases may be unfairly penalized, not for its linguistic quality but for its surface divergence.

The consequences of this shift extend beyond individual metrics. Evaluation now shapes the incentives that drive NLP research: models are optimized for the scores that current benchmarks reward, not necessarily for the linguistic adequacy or interpretability that human

J. Park, *Evaluation by Alignment*, Synthesis Lectures on Computer Science,
https://doi.org/10.1007/978-3-032-16563-3_1

users value. When evaluation fails to reflect the underlying structure or meaning of language, it can distort research priorities, making incremental numerical gains appear more significant than substantive advances in modeling.

In this book, we revisit the role of evaluation from this broader perspective. We examine how traditional metrics have served the field, why their assumptions are no longer sufficient for modern NLP, and how a general, alignment-based approach can restore interpretability and robustness. By framing evaluation as a process of aligning linguistic structures rather than matching surface forms, we aim to provide a unified methodology that remains valid across segmentation schemes, annotation conventions, and languages. The following sections trace this evolution in greater detail and introduce the motivation for the JP-framework (short for *jointly preprocessed*), which serves as the foundation for robust and transparent evaluation throughout this book.

1.2 Overview of Major NLP Tasks and Their Standard Evaluation Metrics

Different NLP tasks employ different evaluation metrics depending on the form and granularity of their outputs. The following overview summarizes the dominant practices across levels of analysis.

1.2.1 Segmentation Tasks

Segmentation tasks aim to identify meaningful boundaries within a text, such as words, morphemes, or sentences. They constitute one of the most fundamental stages of linguistic analysis, as all subsequent tasks depend on how text is divided into processable units. **Sentence boundary detection** determines where sentences begin and end, while **tokenization** divides text into word-like units according to language-specific conventions. Both tasks are sensitive to punctuation, orthography, and script, which makes segmentation particularly challenging in languages that lack explicit delimiters, such as Chinese or Thai.

Because segmentation involves identifying the positions of boundaries rather than assigning categorical labels, it is often evaluated as a span-detection problem. Metrics such as **precision**, **recall**, and their harmonic mean, the F_1 **score**, are used to quantify boundary detection quality. A predicted boundary is considered correct if it aligns exactly with a gold boundary; mismatches are counted as false positives or false negatives. This span-based formulation distinguishes between over-segmentation (introducing unnecessary boundaries) and under-segmentation (failing to detect true boundaries), providing a more diagnostic assessment than simple accuracy.

Segmentation evaluation thus reveals not only how many boundaries are placed correctly but also how systematic the system's boundary errors are. This diagnostic property becomes crucial in downstream applications, where even minor segmentation inconsistencies can cascade into significant differences in tagging, parsing, or translation performance.

1.2.2 Tagging Tasks

Tagging tasks assign categorical labels to predefined linguistic units such as words, tokens, or morphemes. They capture the grammatical, morphological, or functional properties of each unit, forming an essential layer between surface segmentation and higher-level syntactic or semantic analysis. Typical examples include **part-of-speech tagging**, where each token is labeled with its syntactic category; **morphological tagging**, which specifies grammatical features such as tense, number, or case; and **functional tagging**, which marks information-structural or discourse roles.

The standard metric for evaluating tagging is **accuracy**, defined as the proportion of correctly predicted tags among all tokens. This measure assumes a one-to-one correspondence between predicted and gold tokens, making it straightforward to compute and interpret when segmentation is consistent. However, tagging accuracy is sensitive to tokenization mismatches: if the system and the reference disagree on how text is segmented, even correct tags may be counted as errors. Despite this limitation, accuracy remains an effective and widely used metric for comparing models trained and evaluated under the same tokenization scheme.

In practice, tagging evaluation provides not only a quantitative measure of labeling quality but also an indirect indicator of a model's linguistic awareness. Since tagging requires distinguishing grammatical categories and morphological patterns, it often serves as a diagnostic task for assessing a model's internal representations of language.

1.2.3 Span-Based Classification Tasks

Span-based classification tasks involve identifying and labeling continuous segments of text that correspond to meaningful linguistic units or semantic roles. Unlike tagging, which assigns one label per token, span-based tasks require detecting both the boundaries and the labels of multi-token expressions. Typical examples include **chunking** (such as noun or verb chunking), which identifies syntactically coherent phrases without specifying their internal structure; **named entity recognition**, which marks spans referring to proper names or entities of specific types; and **semantic role labeling**, which assigns argument roles to spans relative to a predicate.[1]

---

[1] An official standard evaluation script is provided when available; the widely used CoNLL-2000 `conlleval` script is commonly used not only for chunking but also for evaluating named entity recognition and semantic role labeling. The script is accessible at https://www.cnts.ua.ac.be/conll2000/chunking/conlleval.txt.

Evaluation in span-based classification focuses on how accurately the predicted spans match the gold-standard annotations. The standard metrics are **precision**, **recall**, and their harmonic mean, the F_1 **score**. Precision measures the proportion of predicted spans that are correct, while recall measures how many of the reference spans were successfully identified. The F_1 score provides a balanced summary of these two dimensions, ensuring that both under- and over-prediction are penalized.

Different matching criteria can be applied depending on the task. For named entity recognition and chunking, the most common setting requires *exact match* between predicted and gold boundaries. In contrast, semantic role labeling evaluation sometimes allows *partial match* or overlap-based measures, since semantic roles may be expressed through flexible or discontinuous constructions. This flexibility reflects the linguistic diversity of span-based tasks, where the notion of correctness depends on both syntactic boundaries and semantic interpretation.

Overall, span-based classification connects surface segmentation with deeper linguistic structure. It evaluates how well a system can identify meaningful units that go beyond single tokens, bridging the gap between shallow recognition tasks and full syntactic or semantic parsing.

1.2.4 Structure Prediction Tasks

Structure prediction tasks aim to recover the hierarchical organization of a sentence, revealing how words combine to form phrases and how syntactic relations encode grammatical dependencies. Unlike tagging or span-based classification, which operate on local units, structure prediction requires modeling global relations between tokens and spans. The two principal approaches to syntactic structure prediction are dependency parsing and constituency parsing.

Dependency parsing represents a sentence as a set of directed relations between two words, where each token (except the root) depends on a single head. The evaluation of dependency structures relies on two core metrics: the **unlabeled attachment score**, which measures how accurately the parser identifies headâŁ"dependent relations regardless of their labels, and the **labeled attachment score**, which additionally requires that each dependency label match the gold annotation.[2] Conceptually, both UAS and LAS can be viewed as F-scores computed over sets of dependency arcs: the intersection between predicted and gold arcs determines true positives, while missing or spurious arcs correspond to false negatives and false positives. This formulation highlights that dependency evaluation, like other structured prediction metrics, measures the overlap between two relational graphs rather than simple classification accuracy. However, these metrics still assume identical tokenization between the predicted and gold trees. Even a single segmentation mismatch

[2] https://universaldependencies.org/conll18/conll18_ud_eval.py.

can shift the indexing of tokens and invalidate otherwise correct relations, revealing the fragility of dependency evaluation under inconsistent preprocessing.

Constituency parsing instead represents syntactic structure as a hierarchy of nested phrases, reflecting phrase boundaries and syntactic categories. Its evaluation typically uses the **PARSEVAL** metric (Black et al., 1991), implemented in the standard **EVALB** tool, which counts the proportion of correctly predicted constituents relative to the reference tree.[3] The metric reports precision, recall, and the F_1 score of bracket matches, measuring how well the predicted tree reproduces the hierarchical segmentation of the gold annotation. As in dependency parsing, a consistent segmentation between system and reference is essential, since each constituent span is defined by token indices.

Both dependency and constituency evaluation frameworks have become deeply embedded in NLP benchmarking and have shaped decades of syntactic research. However, their reliance on exact token and sentence alignment exposes a broader limitation of traditional metrics. When boundaries differ, evaluation cannot distinguish genuine syntactic errors from mismatched segmentation, which motivates the need for alignment-aware approaches that compare structures independently of surface preprocessing.

1.2.5 Text Generation Tasks

Text generation tasks produce open-form outputs that are not uniquely determined by the input. Systems are expected to generate fluent and semantically faithful text that may vary in length, structure, or phrasing while expressing equivalent meaning. Representative examples include **machine translation** (MT), which converts text from a source to a target language; **text summarization**, which condenses a longer document into a concise form; and **grammatical error correction**, which rewrites learner sentences into linguistically well-formed versions.

Because these outputs can differ in wording while remaining semantically correct, evaluation poses distinctive challenges. Traditional classification metrics such as accuracy or F score are not applicable, since generation outputs may differ in wording even when they convey the same meaning. To address this, generation tasks are commonly evaluated using n-gram overlap measures such as **BLEU** (Papineni et al., 2002), **ROUGE** (Lin, 2004), and **GLEU** (Napoles et al., 2015).[4] These metrics compute precision and recall over overlapping n-grams between the system output and one or more reference texts, and they summarize these overlaps as overall n-gram based scores. They reward lexical similarity and penalize

---

[3] https://nlp.cs.nyu.edu/evalb/.

[4] The original BLEU and ROUGE scripts are no longer accessible from their original URLs. They are available along with other metrics through the repository at https://huggingface.co/evaluate-metric/spaces. The GLEU implementation used in GEC is provided at https://github.com/cnap/gec-ranking. Note that this GLEU is distinct from Google's MT-oriented metric of the same name (Google BLEU).

Table 1.1 Representative NLP tasks and their standard evaluation metrics

Task type	Example tasks	Common metrics
Segmentation	SBD, tokenization	Precision, recall, F_1 score
Tagging	POS tagging, morphological tagging	Accuracy
Span-based classification	NER, chunking, SRL	Precision, recall, F_1 score
Structure prediction	Dependency parsing, constituency parsing	LAS/UAS, PARSEVAL (EVALB)
Text generation	MT, summarization, GEC	BLEU, ROUGE, GLEU

missing or extraneous words, providing a straightforward way to estimate correspondence between generated and reference text.

While convenient and easy to reproduce, n-gram based metrics have important limitations. They are sensitive to superficial variation and often fail to capture deeper syntactic or semantic equivalence. For instance, paraphrases that differ in word choice or sentence structure may be penalized despite preserving meaning, whereas outputs that reuse reference wording without adequate fluency may receive high scores. These limitations have motivated a range of alternative approaches, including embedding-based measures (Yuan et al., 2021; Zhang et al., 2020) and reference-free metrics (Östling et al., 2025), yet n-gram overlap remains the most widely adopted standard for benchmarking generative NLP systems. As in other tasks, their dependence on exact token or sentence alignment underscores the need for evaluation frameworks that can assess correspondence beyond surface form.

1.2.6 Summary of Evaluation Practices

Table 1.1 lists representative NLP tasks and the evaluation metrics typically used for each. Across these tasks, evaluation metrics share a common goal: to quantify how closely system outputs approach human-annotated references. Despite their task-specific formulations, most metrics, whether based on classification accuracy, span overlap, structural matching, or n-gram similarity, ultimately rely on exact correspondence between system output and gold data. This reliance is often implicit yet fundamental, since it presupposes identical sentence segmentation, token boundaries, and annotation conventions. When these assumptions hold, traditional metrics yield consistent and interpretable comparisons. As NLP increasingly adopts integrated, end-to-end architectures and multilingual data, however, such alignment is no longer guaranteed. The next section examines how these assumptions break down in practice and motivates the need for a broader, alignment-aware evaluation framework.

1.3 Limitations of Traditional Evaluation

Although traditional evaluation metrics provide convenient numerical summaries, they share a fundamental assumption: the predicted and reference data must be perfectly aligned at the level of sentences and tokens. This assumption is rarely questioned, yet it underlies nearly all standard evaluation procedures. When preprocessing diverges because of differences in tokenization, sentence segmentation, or normalization, the resulting scores no longer provide a faithful reflection of system performance. What is measured becomes an artifact of formatting rather than a property of linguistic accuracy.

Even small divergences can lead to large discrepancies in reported scores. A single boundary shift may propagate through an entire evaluation pipeline, affecting every subsequent computation. For instance, tokenization mismatches in part-of-speech tagging may be counted as tagging errors even when the labels are linguistically correct. In constituency parsing, segmentation differences can cause otherwise valid trees to be rejected, while in text generation tasks such as machine translation or grammatical error correction, alternative but equally acceptable wordings are penalized under n-gram based metrics like BLEU or GLEU. In each of these cases, the evaluation framework mistakes superficial misalignment for genuine linguistic error.

The problem is not limited to individual tasks but extends to the broader reproducibility of NLP research. Systems trained and evaluated with slightly different preprocessing pipelines may produce incomparable scores, even when their linguistic outputs are similar. This dependency on segmentation and normalization conventions introduces uncontrolled variability, obscuring real progress and complicating cross-lingual comparison. As NLP systems increasingly operate in multilingual and open-domain environments, the fragility of such exact-match evaluation becomes a major obstacle to fair and interpretable assessment.

Addressing these issues requires evaluation methods that can disentangle surface divergence from structural and semantic correspondence. A robust evaluation framework must tolerate differences in preprocessing while preserving sensitivity to genuine linguistic variation. This recognition motivates the need for an **alignment-based approach** that measures similarity at the level of linguistic structure rather than surface form.

1.4 The Need for Robust, Alignment-Aware Evaluation

The limitations of traditional metrics reveal a broader problem in how evaluation is conceived in NLP. To compare systems meaningfully, we require frameworks that tolerate surface variation while maintaining sensitivity to structural and semantic fidelity. Such frameworks must measure linguistic correspondence even when the exact boundaries of tokens, sentences, or phrases differ between system output and gold annotation. They should focus on whether two analyses represent the same underlying structure rather than whether they appear in identical form.

A robust evaluation framework should therefore satisfy three key criteria:

- **Disentangling preprocessing and linguistic errors:** evaluation must distinguish errors arising from tokenization or segmentation mismatches from those reflecting genuine modeling deficiencies;
- **Interpretability and decomposability:** metrics should be transparent, allowing detailed inspection of which aspects of the output contribute to success or failure;
- **Reproducibility across conventions and languages:** evaluation should remain stable under alternative annotation schemes, preprocessing settings, and multilingual data.

Reframing evaluation as a problem of **alignment** offers a principled solution to these challenges. Alignment establishes a correspondence between system and reference representations before scoring, ensuring that evaluation reflects linguistic equivalence rather than surface coincidence. By applying alignment at both sentence and word levels, it becomes possible to compare outputs that differ in segmentation yet convey the same meaning or structure. This alignment-aware perspective provides the conceptual foundation for the `jp`-framework introduced in the following section.

1.5 The JP-Framework: Evaluation by Alignment

This book introduces the JP-framework, a unified and alignment-based approach to evaluation designed to address the shortcomings of traditional metrics. At its core lies the JP-algorithm, which establishes correspondences between system outputs and reference annotations at both the sentence and word levels before any task-specific scoring is applied. This alignment step ensures that evaluation compares equivalent linguistic structures even when their surface forms differ because of tokenization, segmentation, or normalization inconsistencies. By separating the process of alignment from that of scoring, the framework provides a modular foundation applicable to a wide range of NLP tasks.

The JP-framework is implemented through three complementary tools, each targeting a different level of linguistic analysis:

- **JP-PREPROCESSING** to provide robust evaluation for sentence boundary detection and tokenization, aligning system and reference text before computing precision, recall, and F_1 scores (Chap. 3);
- **JP-EVALB** to extend the standard `EVALB` metric for constituency parsing by introducing an alignment layer that reconciles tokenization differences prior to tree comparison (Chap. 4);
- **JP-ERRANT** to refine the evaluation of grammatical error correction by aligning edits across sentences of differing segmentation, enabling fair comparison between system outputs and gold corrections (Chap. 5).

These three tools illustrate how alignment-based evaluation can unify preprocessing, syntactic, and text generation assessment within a single methodological framework. The JP-framework does not replace existing metrics but generalizes them: accuracy, F-score, and BLEU can all be interpreted as special cases of alignment followed by task-specific scoring. This general formulation provides a consistent theoretical basis for evaluating modern NLP systems in a way that remains robust, interpretable, and reproducible across diverse datasets and languages, particularly in end-to-end system evaluation.

1.6 Structure of the Book

The remainder of this book is organized as follows. Chapter 2 introduces the general concept of evaluation by alignment and outlines the motivation for adopting an alignment-based perspective across different natural language processing tasks. Readers who are primarily interested in evaluation methodology rather than algorithmic implementation may skip this chapter without loss of continuity, since its technical details serve mainly as the foundation for later chapters. Chapter 3 presents the core alignment algorithm and demonstrates its application to preprocessing tasks such as tokenization, sentence segmentation, and normalization. Chapter 4 extends the same formulation to syntactic parsing evaluation through JP- EVALB, showing how alignment can account for structural correspondence between predicted and reference trees. Chapter 5 generalizes the framework to grammatical error correction, providing an alignment-based view of edit extraction and comparison between system outputs and gold references. Chapter 6 concludes the book by examining the broader implications of alignment-based evaluation beyond syntactic and correction tasks. It revisits n-gram based metrics for text generation tasks such as machine translation, summarization, and grammatical error correction, and it outlines potential future directions, including multi-reference evaluation strategies that reduce unnecessary penalties for legitimate system outputs under alignment-based evaluation.

The following chapters examine the theoretical properties of the JP-algorithm, including its soundness and correctness, and present empirical evaluations on benchmark datasets across different linguistic domains. These chapters establish a unified framework for robust, alignment-based evaluation in natural language processing, one that measures linguistic correspondence rather than surface similarity.

2 A Joint Preprocessing Framework for Evaluation

2.1 Introduction

Accurate evaluation is a cornerstone of research and development in natural language processing, serving as the foundation for determining whether a system fulfills its intended linguistic or functional goals. Evaluation not only quantifies performance but also shapes the way systems are designed, optimized, and interpreted. In traditional pipelines, evaluation typically involves comparing system outputs against gold standard references through task-specific metrics such as accuracy, precision, recall, or F measures. These methods have proven effective for modular systems, where each component, including tokenization, tagging, parsing, or generation, is evaluated independently to prevent error propagation across stages. Such component-based evaluation frameworks were well suited to earlier generations of language processing systems, where the separation of preprocessing, model inference, and postprocessing was both practical and conceptually clear.

The current landscape of natural language processing has changed substantially. The rapid adoption of end-to-end architectures, particularly those powered by large-scale pretrained models, has blurred the boundaries between preprocessing and downstream analysis. Tasks that once relied on deterministic segmentation and structured intermediate representations are now performed holistically by models that process text as continuous token sequences. These architectures integrate tokenization, tagging, parsing, and generation into a single learning framework, often producing outputs that differ significantly from predefined gold annotations. The flexibility of end-to-end systems introduces new challenges for evaluation, since traditional component-based metrics are not equipped to handle structural mismatches or inconsistencies between reference and hypothesis.

One of the most pervasive challenges is the issue of segmentation mismatch. Conventional evaluation metrics often presuppose that the system output and the gold standard share identical sentence and word boundaries. In real-world data, however, this assumption rarely holds. Learner writing, social media text, or automatically transcribed speech can exhibit

J. Park, *Evaluation by Alignment*, Synthesis Lectures on Computer Science,
https://doi.org/10.1007/978-3-032-16563-3_2

variable sentence boundaries, inconsistent punctuation, or nonstandard tokenization. When such discrepancies occur, even a perfectly valid system output may be unfairly penalized because of a simple boundary misalignment. These cases reveal a critical weakness in current evaluation practices: the dependence on preprocessing consistency rather than on actual linguistic equivalence.

To address this problem, we introduce a new evaluation algorithm referred to as the JP-algorithm (jointly preprocessed evaluation algorithm). The JP-algorithm adopts an alignment-based approach that explicitly reconciles discrepancies in segmentation before evaluation is conducted. By realigning the reference and hypothesis at both sentence and word levels, the algorithm ensures that equivalent linguistic content is compared regardless of preprocessing differences. This alignment process is inspired by methods used in machine translation evaluation, where alignment serves as an intermediate representation linking source and target texts. In the context of monolingual evaluation, alignment functions as a corrective layer that standardizes the comparison between system output and gold reference, eliminating superficial mismatches while preserving linguistic structure.

The JP-algorithm thus provides a unified mechanism for improving the robustness and interpretability of evaluation results. It enhances precision and recall calculations by correcting mismatches in boundary segmentation, prevents score distortion caused by tokenization inconsistencies, and produces more stable evaluation results across diverse corpora. Beyond these immediate advantages, the alignment-based perspective also invites a rethinking of what evaluation measures should capture. Rather than assuming a perfect structural match between reference and hypothesis, it allows the evaluation process to focus on syntactic and semantic correspondence, which are ultimately the properties that define linguistic accuracy.

Two case studies illustrate the limitations of conventional metrics and the necessity of the proposed approach. First, in constituency parsing, the PARSEVAL measures (Black et al., 1991) and their implementation in `EVALB` have long served as the standard for comparing predicted parse trees with gold annotations. A constituent is counted as correct when it matches a gold constituent with the same non-terminal symbol and span. This approach has proven reliable for benchmarked corpora such as the Penn Treebank but encounters problems when gold and predicted parses differ in tokenization, punctuation handling, or sentence segmentation. Even minor discrepancies in preprocessing can cause the entire evaluation to fail, yielding artificially low scores despite structurally similar parses. Second, in grammatical error correction, evaluation frameworks such as `errant` with its $F_{0.5}$ scoring (Bryant et al., 2017; Bryant, 2019) face analogous issues. When learner sentences contain irregular boundaries or run-on constructions, system outputs that split or merge sentences differently are penalized even when the corrections themselves are linguistically appropriate. These examples demonstrate that traditional evaluation metrics tend to conflate segmentation consistency with correction quality, obscuring the true performance of the underlying system.

The contributions of this work are threefold. First, it presents an alignment-based evaluation algorithm that performs joint preprocessing of system and reference texts, enabling reliable comparisons regardless of boundary inconsistencies. Second, it extends the applicability of this framework across several core NLP tasks, including preprocessing evaluation, syntactic parsing, and grammatical error correction. Third, it emphasizes the practical importance of this approach in real-world applications, where linguistic variability and unstructured input data are the norm rather than the exception. The JP-algorithm provides a principled foundation for evaluating such data without imposing unrealistic assumptions about segmentation uniformity.

From a broader perspective, this framework also contributes to the theoretical understanding of evaluation. It formalizes evaluation as a form of alignment, where the objective is not merely to count matches and mismatches but to define a correspondence function between two structured representations. This generalization reveals a deeper connection between evaluation metrics used in different areas of NLP, from syntactic parsing to text generation, and suggests a unifying view in which accuracy, F score, and BLEU-like measures can all be interpreted as instances of alignment followed by task-specific scoring. The alignment step becomes the bridge that links diverse evaluation paradigms under a single theoretical framework.

In summary, the jointly preprocessed evaluation algorithm provides both a practical and conceptual advance in how NLP systems are evaluated. By resolving mismatches in preprocessing and aligning reference and system outputs before scoring, it enables evaluations that reflect linguistic equivalence rather than superficial similarity. The approach applies equally well to parsing, grammatical error correction, and other end-to-end systems, offering a coherent and theoretically grounded foundation for the next generation of evaluation methodologies.

2.2 Algorithms

The jointly preprocessed JP alignment algorithm provides a unified, pattern-based procedure for aligning sentence or word sequences in a monolingual context. It serves as the computational core of the JP-framework, enabling consistent alignment-based evaluation across preprocessing and end-to-end tasks. The algorithm operates by incrementally comparing two input sequences and grouping locally unmatched segments until they satisfy a defined alignment predicate. Algorithm 1 presents the general procedure.

Input $\mathcal{L}$ and $\mathcal{R}$ are unaligned sequences, each represented as an ordered list of sentences or words.

Output $\mathcal{L}'$ and $\mathcal{R}'$ are aligned sequences such that their lengths are equal, i.e., $\text{LEN}(\mathcal{L}') = \text{LEN}(\mathcal{R}')$.

$\mathcal{L}$ and $\mathcal{R}$ denote ordered lists of sentences or words, depending on whether sentence-level or word-level alignment is being performed. The resulting sequences $\mathcal{L}'$ and $\mathcal{R}'$ are aligned such that

$$\text{LEN}(\mathcal{L}') = \text{LEN}(\mathcal{R}').$$

Algorithm 1 JP-alignment (compact pseudo-code)

```
function ALIGNMENT(𝓛, 𝓡):
  𝓛′ ← [ ]; 𝓡′ ← [ ]; i ← 1; j ← 1
  m ← |𝓛|; n ← |𝓡|
  while i ≤ m and j ≤ n do
    if MATCHEDCASES(L_i, R_j) then
      𝓛′ ← 𝓛′ + [L_i]; 𝓡′ ← 𝓡′ + [R_j]
      i ← i + 1; j ← j + 1
    else
      L* ← [ ]; R* ← [ ]
      while i ≤ m and j ≤ n and not MATCHEDCASES(L_{i+1}, R_{j+1}) do
        if REMAININGLEN(𝓛, i) > REMAININGLEN(𝓡, j) then
          L* ← L* + L_i; i ← i + 1
        else
          R* ← R* + R_j; j ← j + 1
        end if
      end while
      𝓛′ ← 𝓛′ + L*; 𝓡′ ← 𝓡′ + R*
    end if
  end while
  return 𝓛′, 𝓡′
```

The predicate $\text{MATCHEDCASES}_{(i,j)}$ determines whether the current pair (L_i, R_j) satisfies the alignment condition:

$$\text{MATCHEDCASES}(L_i, R_j) \iff \begin{cases} L_{i\not\sqcup} = R_{j\not\sqcup} & \text{or} \\ d(L_{i\not\sqcup}, R_{j\not\sqcup}) \geq \delta \text{ and } d(L_{(i+1)\not\sqcup}, R_{(j+1)\not\sqcup}) \geq \delta & \end{cases} \tag{2.1}$$

where $X_{\not\sqcup}$ denotes the string obtained from X after removing all whitespace characters (punctuation is preserved), d is a normalized length distance in $[0, 1]$, and δ is a predefined similarity threshold. The first condition $L_{i\not\sqcup} = R_{j\not\sqcup}$ requires that the left and right elements become identical once whitespace is removed. The second condition states that if they do not match exactly, they must still be sufficiently similar, that is, $d(L_{i\not\sqcup}, R_{j\not\sqcup}) \geq \delta$, and their subsequent elements $s(L_{(i+1)\not\sqcup}, R_{(j+1)\not\sqcup})$ must also either match exactly or satisfy the same similarity requirement.[1]

[1] This MATCHEDCASES predicate applies uniformly to both sentence-level and word-level alignment, and it can be slightly modified for different applications to adapt to the requirements of each task.

2.2.1 Sentence Alignment

For the SENTENCEALIGNMENT procedure, the input and output are defined as follows:

Input: $\mathcal{L}$ and $\mathcal{R}$, representing lists of sentences.
Output: $\mathcal{L}'$ and $\mathcal{R}'$, representing aligned lists of sentences with equal lengths.

We designate two input sets, $\mathcal{L}$ (gold data) and $\mathcal{R}$ (system outputs), where

$$\mathcal{L} = [L_1, L_2, \ldots, L_m], \qquad \mathcal{R} = [R_1, R_2, \ldots, R_n].$$

After alignment, the outputs become, for example,

$$\mathcal{L}' = [[L_1], [L_2, L_3], \ldots, [L_m]], \qquad \mathcal{R}' = [[R_1, R_2], [R_3], \ldots, [R_n]],$$

such that $\text{LEN}(\mathcal{L}') = \text{LEN}(\mathcal{R}')$.

We define two cases for the predicate $\text{MATCHEDCASES}_{(i,j)}$ in sentence alignment:

$$\begin{cases} L_{i\not\sqcup} = R_{j\not\sqcup} \\ (L_{i\not\sqcup} \simeq R_{j\not\sqcup}) \wedge (L_{(i+1)\not\sqcup} = R_{(j+1)\not\sqcup} \vee L_{(i+1)\not\sqcup} \simeq R_{(j+1)\not\sqcup}) \end{cases} \tag{2.2}$$

The operator $\not\sqcup$ denotes the removal of all whitespace characters from a string while preserving punctuation. The condition $L_{i\not\sqcup} = R_{j\not\sqcup}$ in Eq. (2.2) captures cases of exact equality after whitespace removal, while

$$(L_{i\not\sqcup} \simeq R_{j\not\sqcup}) \wedge \left(L_{(i+1)\not\sqcup} = R_{(j+1)\not\sqcup} \vee L_{(i+1)\not\sqcup} \simeq R_{(j+1)\not\sqcup}\right)$$

extends the condition to near matches, allowing local discrepancies between neighboring sentences. These cases together are equivalent to the general predicate defined in Eq. (2.1).

Simply removing spaces may not suffice, since tokenization often introduces or omits grammatical morphemes that do not appear in the gold sentence. To accommodate such cases, alignment also considers pairs whose character sequences $L_{i\not\sqcup}$ and $R_{j\not\sqcup}$ are sufficiently close in length, provided that L_{i+1} and R_{j+1} satisfy the same condition.

The normalized *length distance* $d(L_i, R_j)$ based on character length is defined as:

$$d(L_i, R_j) = 2 \times \frac{|\text{LEN}(L_{i\not\sqcup}) - \text{LEN}(R_{j\not\sqcup})|}{\text{LEN}(L_{i\not\sqcup}) + \text{LEN}(R_{j\not\sqcup})}, \tag{2.3}$$

where LEN returns the number of characters. The value of d ranges from 0 (identical lengths) to 2 (maximal difference). Two sequences are considered alignable when $d(L_i, R_j) \geq \delta$, where δ is a predefined threshold that controls tolerance to length variation.

These two conditions define the sentence matching criteria. If L_i and R_j cannot be aligned, the algorithm concatenates either $\{L_i, L_{i+1}\}$ or $\{R_j, R_{j+1}\}$ based on their relative lengths and repeats the process until the matching condition is satisfied.

2.2.2 Word Alignment

The WORDALIGNMENT algorithm follows the same logical structure as sentence alignment but operates at the word level. Its input and output are defined as follows:

Input: l and r, representing lists of words.
Output: l' and r', representing aligned lists of words with equal lengths.

After alignment, the outputs may take the form

$$l' = [[l_1], [l_2, l_3], \ldots, [l_m]], \qquad r' = [[r_1, r_2], [r_3], \ldots, [r_n]],$$

such that $\text{LEN}(l') = \text{LEN}(r')$. The algorithm accumulates words in l' and r' whenever a direct pair (l_i, r_j) fails to match, which typically occurs because of tokenization mismatches between the system output and the gold reference. Throughout this description, we treat $\mathcal{L}$ and $\mathcal{R}$ in sentence alignment as interchangeable with l_i and r_j in word alignment.

We define two cases for the predicate $\text{MATCHEDCASES}_{(i,j)}$ in word alignment:

$$\begin{cases} l_i = r_j \\ (l_i \neq r_j) \ \wedge \ (l_{i+1} = r_{j+1}) \end{cases} \tag{2.4}$$

When deciding whether to accumulate the next token from l_{i+1} or r_{j+1} in the event of a word mismatch, the decision is based on the remaining sequence lengths rather than on a direct comparison between the current token lengths $\text{LEN}(l_i)$ and $\text{LEN}(r_j)$. The condition is defined as:

$$\big(\text{LEN}(l) - \text{LEN}(l_{0..i})\big) > \big(\text{LEN}(r) - \text{LEN}(r_{0..j})\big),$$

where $\text{LEN}(l_{0..i})$ and $\text{LEN}(r_{0..j})$ denote the cumulative lengths of all tokens up to indices i and j, respectively. If the remaining length on the left side is greater, the algorithm accumulates the next token from l_{i+1}; otherwise, it accumulates from r_{j+1}.

For word-aligned sentence pairs, all words are re-indexed after sentence alignment. Suppose two sentences $[S_i, S_j]$ are merged into a single sequence through alignment, where $S_i = [w_1, w_2, \ldots, w_m]$ and $S_j = [w_1, w_2, \ldots, w_n]$. After concatenation, their indices become

$$[w_1, w_2, \ldots, w_m, w_{m+1}, w_{m+2}, \ldots, w_{m+n}],$$

ensuring that each word in the aligned sentences receives a distinct index.

In cases where multiple words are concatenated within a sentence, indices are re-assigned accordingly. For example, if two words $[w_i, w_j]$ are combined in a sequence such as

$$[\ldots, [w_{i-1}], [w_i, w_j], [w_{j+1}], \ldots],$$

the re-indexed form becomes

$$[\ldots, [w_{(i-1)}], [w_{(i,1)}, w_{(i,2)}], [w_{(j)}], \ldots],$$

where $w_{(i,1)}$ and $w_{(i,2)}$ denote the re-indexed word tokens occupying the ith position in the aligned tuple.

As a result, both the aligned sentence lists L' and R' contain an equal number of sentence groups, and the aligned word lists l' and r' contain an equal number of word groups after re-indexing.

2.2.3 Proof Sketch of Soundness and Correctness

We define a perfect sentence alignment pair as one in which the concatenated strings are identical after removing spaces, that is, $L_{\not{\sqcup}} = R_{\not{\sqcup}}$. If the alignment process merges multiple sentences, cumulative sequences L' and R' are obtained such that the goal condition $L'_{\not{\sqcup}} = R'_{\not{\sqcup}}$ holds at termination. The objective is to show that the algorithm is both *sound* (it never produces invalid alignments) and *correct* (it always terminates with a valid aligned output).

2.2.3.1 Invariants

Throughout the execution of Algorithm 1, the following invariants hold.

Invariant I1 (alignment coverage). At each iteration, the algorithm maintains cumulative coverage of the input sequences:

$$L' = \text{concat}(L_{1..i^*}), \qquad R' = \text{concat}(R_{1..j^*}),$$

where i^* and j^* denote the current coverage indices in the left and right sequences, respectively. All elements up to these indices have either been matched or grouped for subsequent matching.

Invariant I2 (space-removed equality after a match). Whenever a MATCHEDCASES instance is accepted, the algorithm enforces

$$L'_{\not{\sqcup}} = R'_{\not{\sqcup}},$$

for the newly appended segments. This invariant ensures that every aligned pair satisfies either exact equality after whitespace removal or the bounded-distance condition $d(L_i, R_j) \geq \delta$, where d is the normalized length distance defined earlier.

2.2.3.2 Progress and Termination

At each iteration, at least one of the indices i^* or j^* increases as the algorithm advances through the input sequences. Because the number of sentences in both L and R is finite, this monotonic progress prevents infinite looping. Consequently, the algorithm must terminate after a finite number of steps, once all input sentences have been consumed into the aligned outputs L' and R'.

2.2.3.3 Correctness

When the algorithm terminates, all input elements have been fully processed into cumulative sequences L' and R'. By Invariant I2, every aligned segment satisfies the match predicate, either exact equality or the distance condition $d(L_i, R_j) \leq \delta$. At termination:

$$\text{LEN}(L'_{\not\triangle}) = \text{LEN}(R'_{\not\triangle}),$$

and for each aligned pair k,

$$L_{k,\not\triangle} = R_{k,\not\triangle} \quad \text{or} \quad d(L_k, R_k) \geq \delta.$$

Thus, L' and R' are correctly aligned according to the algorithm's defined criteria.

2.2.3.4 Soundness

By construction, the algorithm never aligns two segments that violate the match condition. Each merge operation is applied only when the predicate

$$(L_{i\not\triangle} = R_{j\not\triangle}) \quad \text{or} \quad d(L_i, R_j) \geq \delta$$

holds true. As a result, every alignment step preserves the validity of the matching relation, and no invalid pair can appear in the output. This property establishes the soundness of the algorithm.

2.3 Summary

This chapter presented a joint preprocessing framework for robust and accurate evaluation of NLP systems, with particular emphasis on segmentation-sensitive tasks such as constituency parsing and grammatical error correction. By introducing the JP-algorithm, an alignment-based method operating at both sentence and word levels, we addressed persistent challenges caused by mismatches in tokenization and sentence boundaries. The algorithm preserves alignment integrity through transformations that are formally sound and correct, and its empirical effectiveness was demonstrated using the W&I development dataset in Appendix A. The jointly preprocessed evaluation framework thus establishes a principled and practical foundation for evaluating end-to-end NLP architectures, ensuring that system outputs are compared meaningfully against gold-standard references. Subsequent chapters instantiate this framework in task-specific evaluators, including JP- PREPROCESSING for preprocessing tasks, JP- EVALB for parsing, and JP- ERRANT for grammatical error correction.

2.4 Limitations and Notes

The JP-algorithm is designed specifically for monolingual alignment at the sentence and word levels. Its purpose within the jointly preprocessed framework is to reconcile segmentation differences before evaluation, ensuring that system outputs and gold references are compared on equivalent structural units. The pattern-based procedure introduced in this chapter provides a simple and effective alignment strategy for this setting, and our comparison in Appendix A shows that it performs more reliably than the Gale–Church algorithm in monolingual scenarios.

It is important to note, however, that the pattern-based alignment component of the JP-algorithm is not intrinsic to the framework. Any sentence alignment algorithm can, in principle, replace the current method, as long as it supports the same jointly preprocessed workflow by producing aligned sentence pairs prior to evaluation. The framework does not require a specific alignment model and remains compatible with alternative approaches.

The same flexibility applies to word-level alignment. One could imagine using Levenshtein-style edit distance or IBM-model alignment as substitutes. Levenshtein alignment, however, presupposes linear edit operations and cannot handle non-linear reordering, while IBM-model alignment requires probabilistic prediction based on a trained model. In contrast, the current pattern-based method operates deterministically and does not depend on any pretrained parameters. Nevertheless, any alternative alignment algorithm may be adopted in place of the present one, provided that it preserves the goal of joint preprocessing before the actual evaluation step.

The JP-framework should therefore be understood not as a commitment to a particular alignment algorithm but as a general methodology for ensuring that evaluation is carried out on structurally comparable units. The alignment procedure presented in this chapter serves as one practical instantiation of this idea rather than as a fixed component of the framework.

JP-Preprocessing 3

3.1 Introduction

Preprocessing forms the foundation of natural language processing, transforming raw text into linguistically meaningful units that can be interpreted by higher level models. Two of its most essential components are tokenization, which divides text into words or morphemes, and sentence boundary detection, which identifies where sentences begin and end. These tasks rarely take center stage in research, yet every downstream system, from part-of-speech tagging to syntactic parsing and machine translation, presumes that preprocessing has already been done correctly.

At first glance, **tokenization** may appear straightforward, especially for languages in which words are separated by whitespace and punctuation. This apparent simplicity, however, conceals a deeper complexity. In agglutinative languages such as Korean, Turkish, or Finnish, a single written word may consist of several morphemes that together express grammatical relationships. Tokenization in such languages often requires morphological segmentation, ensuring that functional and inflectional markers are separated and thus accessible to syntactic and semantic analysis. Decisions about how to segment text therefore go beyond technical convenience: they embody theoretical assumptions about what counts as a meaningful linguistic unit and can shape all subsequent analyses.

Sentence boundary detection presents a different kind of difficulty. Punctuation marks such as periods, question marks, or exclamation marks are strong cues, but they are not unambiguous. A period may close a sentence, or instead indicate an abbreviation, a decimal number, or an ordinal. To resolve this ambiguity, many systems treat the task as a classification problem. It is useful to distinguish between **sentence boundary disambiguation**, which decides whether punctuation truly ends a sentence, and **sentence boundary detection** (SBD) more broadly, which must find sentence divisions even when punctuation is unreliable or absent, as in automatic speech recognition transcripts, historical corpora, or social media text (Lim & Park, 2024; Palmer & Hearst, 1997; Reynar & Ratnaparkhi, 1997).

J. Park, *Evaluation by Alignment*, Synthesis Lectures on Computer Science,
https://doi.org/10.1007/978-3-032-16563-3_3

Despite these conceptual and linguistic intricacies, both tokenization and sentence boundary detection are often regarded as solved. Widely available preprocessing pipelines, whether rule based, statistical, or neural, are routinely reused across corpora and languages with little examination. This widespread reuse creates an illusion of robustness. In reality, hidden errors persist, particularly under domain shift or across language families. Because evaluation practices for preprocessing remain underdeveloped and weakly standardized, segmentation mismatches are frequently dismissed as noise, even when they degrade downstream accuracy by fragmenting syntactic structures or misaligning semantic roles.

Previous studies have drawn attention to these issues. For tokenization, Dridan and Oepen (2012) documented systematic differences among systems; for sentence boundary detection, Read et al. (2012) analyzed the limitations of both rule based and statistical approaches. These works provided valuable empirical insights but generally relied on task specific comparisons and lacked a unified framework for evaluating preprocessing across languages and corpora. As a result, there remains no broadly adopted methodology for diagnosing how segmentation mismatches affect higher level processing.

Even the traditional separation between tokenization and sentence segmentation is increasingly difficult to maintain. Both involve identifying boundaries within a continuous character stream and are subject to similar sources of ambiguity. Recognizing this, previous studies have proposed unified character level sequence labeling models that predict both token and sentence boundaries jointly (Evang et al., 2013). While such models perform well on heterogeneous data, their evaluation still inherits the same weaknesses: standard metrics overlook structural mismatches, and comparisons across systems are often confounded by inconsistent annotation schemes.

In this chapter, we argue that the central challenge lies not in the models themselves but in how their outputs are assessed. Existing evaluation metrics fail to account for alignment-based mismatches in segmentation, leading to miscounted matches and overlooked discrepancies. To address this problem, we propose an alignment-based evaluation framework for tokenization and SBD. Drawing on techniques originally developed for machine translation, the framework detects, reconciles, and scores segmentation mismatches in a principled way. It illuminates errors that conventional methods obscure and establishes a more rigorous foundation for evaluating preprocessing in natural language processing. This chapter develops this proposal in a structured way. We begin by examining the linguistic and methodological foundations of preprocessing (Sect. 3.2), outlining how tokenization and sentence boundary detection are carried out and how their outputs have traditionally been evaluated. We then turn to systematic evidence of segmentation mismatches (Sect. 3.3), showing how current metrics obscure many forms of structural divergence. Building on these observations, the chapter introduces an alignment-based evaluation framework that reconciles system and gold segmentations at both the sentence and word levels (Sect. 3.4). The core algorithm is presented along with illustrative examples, followed by case studies demonstrating how alignment-based evaluation performs on English and multilingual corpora (Sect. 3.5). The chapter concludes with a discussion of remaining challenges and clarifies the broader implications of adopting alignment as the basis for preprocessing evaluation (Sect. 3.6).

3.2 Preprocessing and Its Evaluation

Preprocessing is the first step in natural language processing, where a sequence of raw characters in a document is segmented into smaller linguistic units and organized into sentences. This stage typically involves two fundamental tasks: tokenization, which divides text into words, numbers, and punctuation marks, and sentence boundary detection (or disambiguation), which determines where sentences begin and end. Although often considered routine, these steps underpin nearly all higher-level analyses, from part-of-speech tagging and syntactic parsing to semantic interpretation and discourse processing. Accurate preprocessing is crucial, as errors in tokenization or sentence segmentation can propagate through the pipeline, compounding mistakes in downstream tasks. The following subsections examine the principles, methods, and evaluation practices for tokenization and sentence boundary detection.

3.2.1 Tokenization

Tokenization is one of the most fundamental preprocessing steps in natural language processing. It refers to the task of breaking a continuous stream of text into distinct meaning units, or *tokens* (Kaplan, 2005). These tokens typically correspond to words, numbers, or punctuation marks. Despite its apparent simplicity, tokenization is rarely treated as a core NLP task in its own right (Dridan & Oepen, 2012). Instead, it is often assumed to be a solved problem and handled implicitly through standard scripts or tools. Yet tokenization decisions have far-reaching consequences, as they affect every downstream level of linguistic analysis, from part-of-speech tagging and parsing to machine translation and information extraction.

Tokenization in practice. A concrete example illustrates how tokenization shapes the data used in NLP tasks. Consider the Wall Street Journal text from the Penn Treebank (PTB) (Marcus et al., 1993):

(1) *The luxury auto maker last year sold 1,214 cars in the U.S. Howard Mosher, president and chief executive officer, said he anticipates growth for the luxury auto maker in Britain and Europe, and in Far Eastern markets.*

When tokenized under Penn Treebank conventions, surface forms are often segmented in ways that diverge from standard orthography. Numbers, abbreviations, commas, and final periods may be split depending on context, yielding strings such as *1,214*, *U.S.*, or *Mosher* ⊔ , where ⊔ marks the token boundary. These choices are deliberate: they promote consistency across the treebank and ensure that terminal nodes in parse trees align with stable, reproducible token units.

Penn Treebank conventions. The Penn Treebank established the *de facto* standard tokenization scheme for English, which remains widely used today. The distribution of raw text and parsed trees is accompanied by documentation and a simple `sed` script for applying Penn Treebank-style tokenization.[1] This tokenizer follows several principles:

- Most punctuation marks are split from adjoining words.
- Quotation marks are normalized, converting double quotes into paired backticks and apostrophes.
- Verb contractions and genitive markers are segmented into component morphemes, allowing each to be separately tagged in parsing. For instance: *children's* is tokenized as *children* ⊔ *'s*, *parents'* as *parents* ⊔ *'*, *I'm* as *I* ⊔ *'m*, *won't* as *wo* ⊔ *n't*.

These conventions ensure consistency across the treebank and facilitate reliable syntactic annotation.

This design reflects the treebank's annotation philosophy, implemented through simple replacement rules: morphemes are represented in ways that facilitate syntactic analysis. For example, in the phrase *I'm*, the pronoun *I* functions as the subject noun phrase, while the contracted verb *'m* serves as the head of the main verb phrase. The PTB tokenizer, however, assumes that sentence boundaries have already been determined and therefore does not split final periods from abbreviations unless sentence segmentation has been applied in advance.

Alternative tokenization tools. While Penn Treebank conventions have become widely accepted, other systems have developed their own tokenization scripts, either defining distinct criteria or adapting the PTB scheme.

- *Moses*. The statistical machine translation system Moses (Koehn et al., 2007) includes a preprocessing pipeline with scripts for tokenization, punctuation normalization, and truecasing. The tokenization component introduces rules for non-breaking prefixes such as `Mr.`, `Dr.`, or `Bldg.`, which prevent erroneous sentence splits. Truecasing reduces data sparsity by converting the initial words of sentences to their most probable casing, thereby producing more consistent training data for machine translation.
- *Stanford CoreNLP*. CoreNLP (Manning et al., 2014) provides a general-purpose NLP toolkit in which tokenization is integrated with part-of-speech tagging, syntactic parsing, named entity recognition, and other modules. Its tokenizer largely follows PTB conventions but introduces some differences: for example, it does not always separate periods in abbreviations such as *U.S.*, treating the entire string as a single token rather than splitting it into *U* ⊔ . ⊔ *S* ⊔.

[1] ftp://ftp.cis.upenn.edu/pub/treebank/public_html/tokenizer.sed.

These examples illustrate how even widely used systems diverge in systematic ways, underscoring that tokenization cannot be treated as a mere technicality. Because tokenization is often taken for granted, its methodological significance has been underestimated, a point that becomes especially clear when considering how such mismatches are evaluated.

Evaluation on tokenization. The evaluation of tokenization quality has often been framed in terms of the Levenshtein distance (LD), where system output is compared against gold-standard tokenization. Dridan and Oepen (2012) propose the use of the Levenshtein distance as a straightforward measure of divergence between tokenization schemes. In their study, tokenization results were compared against the Penn Treebank reference, using Sections 03–06 of the Wall Street Journal portion as the evaluation set.

The Levenshtein distance provides a way to quantify how many elementary edits (insertions, deletions, or substitutions) are needed to transform the system tokens into the gold segmentation. Applied to tokenization, this measure captures even small but systematic mismatches, such as differences in punctuation splitting or abbreviation handling. Figure 3.1 illustrates this with an example from `tokenizer.sed`, where the system output diverges from the gold standard in its treatment of numbers and abbreviations. Although such discrepancies appear minor, they can propagate through later processing and influence syntactic or semantic analysis.

For instance, a system that produces 1 ⊔ , ⊔ 214 and U ⊔ . ⊔ S ⊔ . instead of the Penn Treebank forms *1214* and *U.S.* incurs an edit cost of five. This reflects the five additional characters needed to reconcile the two representations, yielding $LD = 5$.

This approach highlights that tokenization discrepancies, while often subtle, accumulate into measurable distance from the reference standard. It provides a principled way of evaluating tokenization methods not just qualitatively but quantitatively, by aligning system output to canonical conventions and recording the minimal operations required to correct it. As such, edit distance offers an informative, corpus-level metric for assessing tokenization consistency and robustness.

In tokenization evaluation, precision and recall are defined analogously to their use in information retrieval. Precision measures the proportion of system-produced tokens that are correct, while recall measures the proportion of gold-standard tokens that the system successfully identifies. Because tokenization systems may over-segment or under-segment text, both precision and recall are important for capturing different kinds of errors. The F_1-score is then used as a balanced measure that combines these two aspects:

GOLD: The luxury auto maker last year sold 1,214 cars in the U.S.
SYSTEM: The luxury auto maker last year sold 1 ⊔ , ⊔ 214 cars in the U ⊔ . ⊔ S ⊔ .

Fig. 3.1 Example of tokenization mismatches: gold segmentation vs. `tokenizer.sed` output, highlighting differences in number and abbreviation handling

$$\text{Precision} = \frac{\text{relevant tokens} \cap \text{retrieved tokens}}{\text{retrieved tokens}} \tag{3.1}$$

$$\text{Recall} = \frac{\text{relevant tokens} \cap \text{retrieved tokens}}{\text{relevant tokens}} \tag{3.2}$$

$$F_1 = 2 \cdot \frac{\text{Precision} \cdot \text{Recall}}{\text{Precision} + \text{Recall}} \tag{3.3}$$

In the example above, the system produces 17 tokens, of which 10 align with the gold segmentation. The gold standard contains 12 tokens in total, yielding a precision of $\frac{10}{17}$ and a recall of $\frac{10}{12}$. Substituting these values into the formula gives an F_1 score of approximately 0.67. Although the system captures most of the gold tokens, its tendency to over-segment reduces precision and thereby lowers the overall score.

3.2.2 SBD

Sentence boundary detection (SBD), sometimes referred to as sentence boundary disambiguation in the context of written text, is another essential component of preprocessing. Its role is to determine where sentences begin and end, thereby enabling sentence-level processing tasks such as part-of-speech tagging, chunking, and syntactic parsing. In automatic speech recognition, the term *sentence boundary detection* is generally used, while in written text processing the task is more accurately described as *sentence boundary disambiguation*, since the challenge often lies in deciding whether a punctuation mark–typically a period–signals the end of a sentence or merely marks an abbreviation.

SBD in practice. In early work, SBD was typically cast as a binary classification problem: at each occurrence of a period, the system must decide whether it marks the end of a sentence or not. Studies such as Palmer and Hearst (1997) and Reynar and Ratnaparkhi (1997) approached the task with statistical classifiers that focused on distinguishing full stop punctuation from periods marking abbreviations. Later, Gillick (2009) advanced this line of work by framing SBD as a supervised learning problem in which features are extracted from the tokens immediately to the left (L) and right (R) of the candidate period. These context-sensitive features, including word identity, token length, and capitalization, are then used to predict the presence of a sentence boundary.

Gillick (2009) implemented this approach in the system SPLITTA,[2] which employed both Naïve Bayes and Support Vector Machine classifiers. Experimental results demonstrated significant gains over previous methods: while earlier systems such as MXTERMINATOR (Reynar & Ratnaparkhi, 1997) achieved around 98% accuracy on the Wall Street Journal corpus, SPLITTA reduced error rates to below 0.8%. Crucial to these improvements was the observation that certain contextual features are highly informative. For example, the length of the token preceding a period proved to be a reliable proxy for distinguishing abbreviations

[2] https://github.com/dgillick/splitta.

from sentence-final words, and the capitalization of the following token offered a strong signal for sentence-initial position.

Despite these successes, SBD remains a subtle task due to the interaction between punctuation conventions, abbreviations, and formatting inconsistencies. Corpus-level experiments have also shown that results vary across genres: training on the Brown corpus, which represents diverse written registers, and the Poe corpus, which includes prose and poetry, helped improve robustness when applied to Wall Street Journal texts. These cross-corpus evaluations underline that while sentence boundary disambiguation can be highly accurate in controlled domains, portability across genres is less straightforward.

Overall, research in SBD illustrates how a seemingly simple preprocessing step involves nuanced linguistic considerations and domain-specific variation. It also shows how classification-based approaches, when supported by carefully designed features, can push accuracy toward near-human levels while still revealing the limits of punctuation-based disambiguation in real-world text.

Evaluation on SBD. Evaluation of sentence boundary detection has traditionally been carried out using **error rate**, defined as the proportion of incorrectly classified periods over the total number of ambiguous periods (Gillick, 2009; Read et al., 2012). This metric reflects the fact that sentence boundaries in written text are most often marked by periods, which must be disambiguated from abbreviations such as *U.S.* or *Inc.*. For example, consider the sentence *The luxury auto maker last year sold 1,214 cars in the U.S. Howard Mosher* ··· in (3.2.1). If a system incorrectly labels the period in ··· *U.S.* as not a sentence boundary[3] but correctly detects the period after ··· *markets.*, the resulting error rate is $\frac{1}{2}$, since one of the two ambiguous periods is misclassified.

More generally, standard classification metrics such as accuracy, precision, recall, and the F_1-score are widely used. Accuracy reflects the overall proportion of correctly identified boundaries, typically defined as accuracy = 1 − error rate, while precision and recall capture the tradeoff between false positives (incorrectly predicting a boundary) and false negatives (failing to detect a true boundary):

$$\text{Precision} = \frac{\text{relevant sentences} \cap \text{retrieved sentences}}{\text{retrieved sentences}} \tag{3.4}$$

$$\text{Recall} = \frac{\text{relevant sentences} \cap \text{retrieved sentences}}{\text{relevant sentences}} \tag{3.5}$$

The F_1 score balances these two, but it can be significantly influenced by how sentences are annotated and segmented–a point we elaborate in the next section.

Evaluation is typically conducted on the Wall Street Journal sections of the Penn Treebank, using the raw-to-annotated alignments provided by Dridan and Oepen (2012). This setup facilitates system comparison and underscores the fact that even a seemingly straight-

[3] Because the final period in *U.S.* may be interpreted either as part of the abbreviation or as the sentence-final marker.

forward preprocessing task like sentence segmentation demands clearly defined and consistent evaluation standards.

3.3 Mismatches in Preprocessing

Preprocessing mismatches arise when the output of tokenization or sentence boundary detection diverges from the intended gold standard. Although such mismatches have been observed and documented in earlier work, they are often underestimated in practice. This is largely due to the prevailing assumption that preprocessing is a solved and standardized step, an assumption that allows subtle but consequential segmentation errors to pass unnoticed. These errors are not merely cosmetic; they distort syntactic and semantic representations, disrupt alignment in multilingual applications, and ultimately degrade the reliability of downstream tasks.

In this section, we address these mismatches not simply to catalog their occurrence, but to develop a principled evaluation method that can account for them. Building on insights from prior comparative studies, we show that existing evaluation practices fail to detect or quantify many forms of structural divergence in preprocessing. To address this gap, we introduce an alignment-based evaluation framework that reconciles system output with gold segmentation through minimal edits. By treating token and sentence boundaries as alignment targets, our method provides a flexible and robust way to identify, measure, and correct segmentation mismatches.

We begin by analyzing tokenization and sentence boundary mismatches across common systems, then assess how standard evaluation metrics fall short. Finally, we demonstrate how alignment-based strategies offer a more accurate and reproducible alternative for evaluating preprocessing performance.

3.3.1 Tokenization Mismatches

Tokenization, while often considered a routine preprocessing step, exhibits persistent inconsistencies across systems. These mismatches arise from divergent handling of contractions, sentence-final periods, and abbreviations, which are treated differently depending on the tokenizer's design principles. Consider the sentence *When No. 1 Isn't the Best.*[4] Three commonly used tokenizers produce the following outputs:

[4] The sentence is extracted from a *Washington Post* article published on May 26, 2004. The original text is available at https://www.washingtonpost.com/archive/sports/2004/05/26/when-no-1-isnt-the-best/fa34156f-881a-4181-b0fe-4447e2f36f0e/.

`tokenizer.sed`	When No ⊔ . 1 is ⊔ n't the Best
`Moses`	When No. 1 isn ⊔ 't the Best
`CoreNLP`	When No. 1 is ⊔ n't the Best

This small example reveals systematic divergences in the treatment of periods and contractions. Periods are especially ambiguous: they can signal sentence boundaries, appear in abbreviations (e.g., *U.S.*), or serve orthographic functions (e.g., *No.*). Tokenizers vary in whether they attach periods to adjacent tokens or isolate them, leading to incompatible outputs even for well-formed English sentences. Likewise, contractions may be segmented in ways that do not reflect their true surface form. For example, *isn't* is often split into *isn* + *'t*, a convention adopted in earlier statistical machine translation systems to reduce data sparsity, whereas *can't* is typically segmented according to its underlying morphological structure as *ca* + *n't*. These decisions are rarely neutral; they reflect differing assumptions about what constitutes a token and what granularity is appropriate for syntactic or semantic analysis.

Though such differences may seem minor, they have nontrivial downstream consequences. In part-of-speech tagging, token boundary mismatches can distort tagging distributions. In parsing, they may misalign syntactic bracketing or dependency heads. In machine translation, mismatched segmentation affects word alignment and translation quality. These problems are exacerbated when corpora processed with different tokenizers are merged or when training and test data follow different segmentation schemes.

Even in English, where the Penn Treebank tokenizer has served as a *de facto* standard, these mismatches remain. While `tokenizer.sed`, Moses, and CoreNLP generally aim to follow Penn Treebank conventions, they differ in implementation details: for example, CoreNLP tends to retain period-attached abbreviations such as *U.S.* as single tokens, whereas `tokenizer.sed` splits them into multiple units. These choices are deliberate, yet inconsistent, and reflect how system-specific heuristics override universal definitions.

The challenges are even more pronounced in morphologically rich languages. In Korean or Turkish, a single orthographic word may encode multiple morphemes, each corresponding to a distinct syntactic or semantic role. Tokenization in such cases is tightly coupled with morphological analysis and varies depending on linguistic theory or application needs. As a result, what counts as a "token" is fundamentally language- and task-dependent.

These observations highlight a critical methodological concern: the assumption that tokenization is a solved or standardized task is misleading. Discrepancies across systems remain widespread and largely unevaluated, despite their implications for model performance. Recognizing and quantifying these mismatches is essential for developing robust, transparent NLP pipelines. As the next section will show, these issues are not confined to token-level segmentation but extend to sentence boundaries as well, underscoring the need for an evaluation framework that explicitly handles structural divergence.

3.3.2 Challenges in SBD

While sentence boundary detection is often guided by terminal punctuation, it remains a persistently error-prone task due to domain variation, punctuation ambiguity, and inconsistent orthographic conventions. Even state-of-the-art systems struggle to segment sentences reliably in the absence of clear punctuation, or when multiple sentences appear within a single orthographic span.

Such mismatches are not rare edge cases but systematic phenomena that surface across a range of corpora. To illustrate, consider the following fragment from the Europarl parallel corpus (Koehn, 2005).

```
Opening of the session
I declare resumed the 2000-2001 session of the European
 Parliament.
Agenda
Mr President, the second item on this morning's agenda
 is the recommendation for second reading on cocoa and
 chocolate products, for which I am the rapporteur. Quite
 by accident I learnt yesterday, at 8.30 p.m., that the
 vote was to take place at noon today.
```

Most sentence splitters, including those that attempt to infer structure beyond punctuation, struggle with this example because several cues that humans rely on are either missing or ambiguous. A human reader can easily identify five sentences, yet an automatic SBD system typically finds only three. One source of difficulty is the absence of sentence-final periods in fragments such as *Opening* ... or *Agenda*, which prevents punctuation-based models from marking clear boundaries. Another source of ambiguity comes from the capitalization of items like *I* and *Mr*, which may signal either the start of a new sentence or a proper noun within an ongoing one. As a result, most SBD tools merge several distinct sentences into larger spans, detecting only the sequence ending in *Parliament.*, the sequence ending in *rapporteur.*, and the final sentence. This shows how subtle gaps and overloads in surface punctuation create genuine challenges for robust sentence boundary detection.

These challenges are amplified in informal or noisy data. In social media posts, users frequently omit punctuation, employ non-standard capitalization, or insert emojis and symbols in syntactically ambiguous locations. In such contexts, sentence boundaries must be inferred from lexical or discourse cues rather than typographic signals. Similarly, automatic speech recognition systems typically produce transcripts devoid of punctuation, making SBD reliant on prosodic and contextual features. To address this, researchers have explored both punctuation restoration as a precursor to SBD (Alam et al., 2020; Fu et al., 2021; Poláček et al., 2023) and direct segmentation models trained on speech-derived corpora (Treviso et al., 2017; González-Gallardo & Torres-Moreno, 2018).

Recent approaches such as character-level sequence labeling (Evang et al., 2013) and linguistically enriched datasets (Lim & Park, 2024) offer more flexible frameworks for boundary prediction, especially in settings where punctuation is unreliable. However, even these models frequently disagree with gold segmentations in subtle ways. Whether due to misaligned boundaries, tokenization inconsistencies, or stylistic variation, the result is the same: mismatches between system outputs and annotated ground truth.

Importantly, such mismatches complicate evaluation. Simple precision and recall metrics fail to account for minor misalignments or structurally equivalent variants, especially when sentence boundaries are not exact matches. As with tokenization, a more nuanced, alignment-based approach is needed to accurately assess SBD performance across diverse data conditions. The following section develops such a framework.

3.3.3 Preprocessing Evaluation Issues

Standard evaluation metrics for tokenization and sentence boundary detection, such as Levenshtein distance, error rate, and precision/recall, have long provided the foundation for assessing segmentation quality. As discussed in the previous section, these methods offer complementary perspectives: edit distance captures local divergence, accuracy and error rate quantify overall classification performance, and precision/recall highlight the trade-offs between over- and under-segmentation.

Despite their widespread adoption, these approaches share a critical limitation: they rely on exact matches between predicted and gold-standard boundaries. As a result, even small deviations in token boundaries or sentence segmentation, such as attachment of punctuation or off-by-one errors, are penalized as harshly as more serious structural mismatches. For instance, a tokenizer that splits at the wrong point by just one character receives the same penalty as one that splits an entirely different word. Similarly, a sentence boundary predicted slightly earlier or later than the gold boundary may be counted as a complete miss.

These rigid evaluation criteria become particularly problematic in real-world settings, where segmentation conventions vary across domains, or where gold standards are inconsistently applied. Under such conditions, current evaluation methods either miscount linguistically acceptable alternatives as errors, or mistakenly reward superficial matches that do not reflect true equivalence in structure or interpretation.

This problem is especially evident in tokenization evaluation. Consider the following example:

GOLD	*This ca* ⊔ *n't be right* ⊔ .
SYSTEM	*This can* ⊔ *not be right* ⊔ .

The gold-standard preserves the contracted form *ca ⊔ n't*, while the system tokenizer restores it to the canonical form *can ⊔ not*. From a linguistic perspective, these forms are syntactically and semantically equivalent. Yet under token-level precision and recall metrics, the system output is penalized for producing the "wrong" token boundaries. This is misleading–particularly when the system is designed to perform normalization, such as lemmatizing contractions or segmenting according to morphosyntactic structure.

These cases highlight a broader challenge: should preprocessing evaluation enforce strict surface-form fidelity, or allow some degree of linguistic equivalence? In downstream tasks such as constituency parsing, exact token alignment is often required by evaluation tools like `EVALB`, which treat any boundary mismatch as disqualifying even when the underlying parse structure is otherwise aligned. In response, some evaluations incorporate token-agnostic alignment or canonicalization layers. However, for preprocessing tasks like tokenization itself, the purpose of evaluation may differ: fidelity to an annotation guideline might take precedence, especially when training data and downstream models expect consistent segmentation schemes.

Further complications arise when tokenization interacts with sentence boundary detection. For example, restoring a contraction to its canonical form may change the number or position of tokens in a sentence, shifting the location of the expected sentence boundary. In this way, a seemingly harmless normalization step may cause evaluation metrics for sentence segmentation to register a false mismatch, even when the boundary itself remains linguistically valid.

Evaluation of sentence boundary detection faces similar challenges. In character-level SBD tasks, such as those discussed by Dridan and Oepen (2012), each character position is treated as a potential sentence boundary point. If a boundary is omitted, it is counted as a false negative. While this framing enables the use of precision, recall, and F1 score, it introduces an imbalance: sentence boundaries are sparse relative to the number of non-boundary positions, making it easy for a naïve model to achieve high accuracy simply by predicting no boundaries.

Character-level representations also struggle to distinguish partial matches from exact ones. Consider the following example, where sentence segmentation is evaluated using BIO-style tagging[5]:

In Fig. 3.2, the system segments the sentence between *Click here* and *To view it.*, producing two sentence boundaries. The gold standard, however, marks only one boundary between *here* and *To*. Although the system boundary is nearly correct, the surrounding structure is not. Traditional BIO-style evaluation may nonetheless treat *Click here* as a correctly detected sentence, which leads to overestimation of precision or recall.

[5] The original BIO scheme marks the beginning and inside of labeled spans. For this illustration it is adapted to an STIO variant so that sentence boundary detection and tokenization can be represented as a character-level sequence labeling task, with `S` indicating sentence boundaries, `T` token boundaries, `I` characters inside a token, and `O` characters outside these spans.

```
     Click here To view it.
SYS  SIIIIOTIIIIOSIOTIIIIOTIT
GOLD SIIIIOTIIIIOTIOTIIIIOTIT
```

Fig. 3.2 BIO-style evaluation in previous work where partially matched sentences (e.g., *Click here*) may be considered `true positives`

These examples show that current evaluation methods for both tokenization and SBD lack robustness in the face of minor structural mismatches or linguistically valid variation. They miscount partial alignments, fail to reflect syntactic or discourse-level equivalence, and often obscure real differences in system behavior.

To overcome these limitations, we propose an alignment-based evaluation framework that identifies minimal transformations between predicted and reference segmentations. Drawing on alignment algorithms from machine translation, our method compares segmentation structures at the boundary level while allowing for structural variation. This enables more accurate, transparent, and linguistically meaningful assessments of preprocessing quality, particularly in multilingual, learner, or noisy text where segmentation inconsistencies are common but often harmless.

3.3.4 Summary of Limitations

Mismatches in tokenization and sentence boundary detection are not edge cases but systematic outcomes of linguistic ambiguity and annotation inconsistency. Existing evaluation metrics, though well established, tend to over-penalize recoverable differences and overlook structural variation. They conflate superficial mismatches with deeper segmentation errors, masking system behavior and hindering fair comparison. These limitations point to the need for an evaluation framework grounded in alignment–one that distinguishes genuine errors from acceptable variation. We introduce such a framework in the next section.

3.4 Alignment-Based Evaluation

To address the limitations of traditional evaluation metrics for tokenization and sentence boundary detection, we adopt an alignment-based evaluation framework. Our approach is inspired by sentence and word alignment techniques widely used in machine translation, where alignments are necessary to reconcile structural differences between source and target languages. In MT, even when sentences are direct translations of each other, they often diverge in word order, length, and syntactic structure—necessitating robust alignment algorithms to support further processing.

While preprocessing evaluation operates in a monolingual setting, it faces a similar structural challenge. System outputs and gold references may contain the same characters in the

INPUT FILE:
```
Click here To view it. He makes some good⊓
observations on a few of the picture's.⊓
```

SYSTEM RESULT:
```
Click here⊓
To view it ⊔ . ⊓
He makes some good observations on a few of the picture ⊔ 's ⊔ . ⊓
```

GOLD FILE:
```
Click here To view it ⊔ . ⊓
He makes some good observations on a few of the picture ⊔ 's ⊔ . ⊓
```

SENTENCE-ALIGNED RESULT FOR PREPROCESSING EVALUATION:
```
Click here ~~~ To view it ⊔ . ⊓          Click here To view it ⊔ . ⊓
He makes some good observations on       He makes some good observations on
a few of the picture ⊔ 's ⊔ . ⊓          a few of the picture ⊔ 's ⊔ . ⊓
```

Fig. 3.3 Intermediate alignment-based evaluation result. The system's two sentences *Click here* and *To view it.* are merged into a single aligned unit to match the gold segmentation. ⊔ denotes token boundaries, ⊓ sentence boundaries, and ~~~ indicates sentence merging via alignment

same order, but differ in how they are segmented into tokens and sentences. These differences can cause one-to-many or many-to-one mappings between lines or token spans, much like cross-language alignment. The core idea behind our method is to reinterpret these preprocessing outputs as sequences to be aligned—not across languages, but across segmentation schemes.

Figure 3.3 illustrates a simplified example of this process. Although the input string is identical across the system and gold files, the sentence boundaries differ: the system segments *Click here* and *To view it.* as two sentences, while the gold file treats them as one. A naïve evaluation would penalize this as a boundary error. However, our alignment algorithm merges these system segments into a single unit that correctly aligns with the gold sentence, resolving the apparent mismatch.

While Fig. 3.3 focuses on sentence boundary detection, the same alignment principle is applicable to tokenization evaluation. In that case, word-level alignment allows us to detect over-segmentation, under-segmentation, and recoverable boundary mismatches–without penalizing outputs that preserve structural equivalence. We develop the full algorithm in the following section.

3.4.1 Algorithm Description

This section provides a brief overview of the alignment procedure used to compare system output with the reference segmentation.

Notations. To describe the proposed alignment algorithm concisely, we introduce the following notations. Let $\mathcal{L}$ and $\mathcal{R}$ denote the system output and the gold-standard file, respectively, each consisting of segmented sentences. We assume that the character sequences are identical across the two files, differing only in tokenization and sentence segmentation.

Let $\mathcal{L}_{\not\sqcup}$ and $\mathcal{R}_{\not\sqcup}$ represent the versions of $\mathcal{L}$ and $\mathcal{R}$ with all token boundary markers ($\sqcup$) removed. We assume $\text{LEN}(\mathcal{L}_{\not\sqcup}) = \text{LEN}(\mathcal{R}_{\not\sqcup})$, meaning that the two files match at the character level.

Let L and R denote a pair of corresponding sentences from $\mathcal{L}$ and $\mathcal{R}$, respectively. For both L and R, we use the following interchangeable terms:

$C_{sb}(\mathcal{L})$ and $C_{tk}(\mathcal{L})$:	The total number of sentence boundaries (sb) and tokens (tk) in $\mathcal{L}$.
$\texttt{TP}_{\texttt{sb}}$ and $\texttt{TP}_{\texttt{tk}}$:	The number of true positives ($\texttt{tp}$) for sentence boundaries and tokens, respectively.
$L_{\sqcup}$:	The version of L in which token boundary markers (i.e., spaces) are preserved.
$L_{\not\sqcup}$:	The version of L with token boundary markers (i.e., spaces) removed.
L_i:	The ith token in $L_{\sqcup}$.

Evaluation measures. To compute the F1 score for sentence boundary detection, we use the total number of sentence boundaries in both the system output and the gold standard, denoted by $Csb(\mathcal{L})$ and $Csb(\mathcal{R})$. We also require the number of true positives for sentence boundaries, denoted by $\texttt{TP}_{\texttt{sb}}$.

Based on these counts, precision and recall are defined as follows:

$$\text{Precision}_{sb} = \frac{\texttt{TP}_{\texttt{sb}}}{C_{sb}(\mathcal{L})} \tag{3.6}$$

$$\text{Recall}_{sb} = \frac{\texttt{TP}_{\texttt{sb}}}{C_{sb}(\mathcal{R})} \tag{3.7}$$

The F1 score is then calculated as the harmonic mean of precision and recall:

$$F_{sb} = 2 \cdot \frac{\text{Precision}_{sb} \cdot \text{Recall}_{sb}}{\text{Precision}_{sb} + \text{Recall}_{sb}} \tag{3.8}$$

The same procedure applies to token-level evaluation, where token boundaries replace sentence boundaries and the resulting score is denoted by F_{tk}.

Sentence alignment for SBD evaluation. The proposed alignment algorithm processes $\mathcal{L}$ and $\mathcal{R}$ and increments the $\texttt{TP}_{sb}$ count whenever $L_{\not\sqcup}$ and $R_{\not\sqcup}$ are identical. When they do not match, the algorithm merges consecutive sentences in L' and R' until the character sequences of the next $L_{\not\sqcup}$ and $R_{\not\sqcup}$ are equal (rather than comparing the cumulative merged strings L' and R' directly). Once alignment is achieved, the algorithm resumes comparison and continues incrementing $\texttt{TP}_{sb}$ whenever the character sequences match.

Word alignment for tokenization evaluation. For token-level evaluation, the algorithm compares word-aligned sentence pairs $L_\sqcup$ and $R_\sqcup$. The $\texttt{TP}_{tk}$ count is incremented whenever the i-th token in $L_\sqcup$ matches the j-th token in $R_\sqcup$, i.e., $L_i = R_j$. While classical IBM word alignment models could be adapted for token alignment, our focus is narrower: we align tokens only within already sentence-aligned pairs, rather than across the entire document. This localized alignment is sufficient for preprocessing evaluation, as it directly captures token equivalence within each matched sentence pair.

Summary. Drawing from the analogy to sentence and word alignment in machine translation, we introduced an alignment-based algorithm for evaluating sentence boundary detection and tokenization. The algorithm operates in a single pass, aligning corresponding sentence and token units, and incrementing true positive counts with high structural sensitivity. This design enables more accurate and unified evaluation of preprocessing outputs, particularly in the presence of segmentation mismatches that traditional metrics fail to capture.

3.4.2 Pseudo-codes

Implementations. We provide two implementations of the alignment-based evaluation procedure: a basic version (Algorithm 1) and a joint version (Algorithm 2).

In Algorithm 1, sentence boundary detection and tokenization are evaluated in separate stages. The first outer `while` loop performs sentence alignment and obtains $\texttt{TP}_{\texttt{sb}}$, and the second outer loop computes $\texttt{TP}_{\texttt{tk}}$ during word alignment. We assume that $N \simeq N'$ and $M \simeq M'$ for the left (L) and right (R) sequences. Here, $L'_{i,i'}$ refers to the i'-th token in the i-th sentence of L'. This two-stage structure is conceptually clear, although it requires two passes over the aligned data.

Algorithm 2 evaluates sentence boundaries and token boundaries within a single loop. The alignment operations and comparisons are the same as in the basic version, and both algorithms therefore share the same asymptotic time complexity of $\mathcal{O}(NM)$. The joint implementation is provided for convenience, since it avoids a second traversal of the aligned sequences and simplifies practical use.

A key difference between the two implementations lies in how alignment information is reused. The basic algorithm aligns sentences first and then performs token alignment on the merged spans created in the previous stage. The joint algorithm performs these two operations simultaneously. This does not change the asymptotic complexity, since both versions compare the same number of boundaries and tokens, but it changes how intermediate structures are maintained. The basic algorithm is easier to inspect step by step, and the joint algorithm is more compact in practice because it does not require storing intermediate aligned sequences.

Algorithm 1 BASIC ALGORITHM

function BASIC ALGORITHM ($\mathcal{L}$, $\mathcal{R}$):
Input: $\mathcal{L}, \mathcal{R}$
Output: $\mathcal{C}_{sb}(\mathcal{L}), \mathcal{C}_{tk}(\mathcal{L}), \mathcal{C}_{sb}(\mathcal{R}), \mathcal{C}_{tk}(\mathcal{R})$, $\texttt{TP}_{\texttt{sb}}$, $\texttt{TP}_{\texttt{tk}}$
Obtain $\mathcal{C}_{sb}(\mathcal{L}), \mathcal{C}_{tk}(\mathcal{L}), \mathcal{C}_{sb}(\mathcal{R})$, and $\mathcal{C}_{tk}(\mathcal{R})$ from $\mathcal{L}$ and $\mathcal{R}$
while $\mathcal{L}$ and $\mathcal{R}$ **do**
  /* Obtain $\texttt{TP}_{\texttt{sb}}$ */
  if $L_{i\not\sqcup} == R_{j\not\sqcup}$ **then**
    $\texttt{TP}_{\texttt{sb}} \leftarrow \texttt{TP}_{\texttt{sb}} + 1$
    $\mathcal{L}', \mathcal{R}' \leftarrow \mathcal{L}' + L_i, \mathcal{R}' + R_j$
  else
    while $L_{i+1\not\sqcup} \neq R_{j+1\not\sqcup}$ **do**
      $L' \leftarrow L' + L_i$
      $R' \leftarrow R' + R_j$
    end while
    $\mathcal{L}', \mathcal{R}' \leftarrow \mathcal{L}' + L', \mathcal{R}' + R'$
  end if
end while
while $\mathcal{L}'$ and $\mathcal{R}'$ **do**
  /* Obtain $\texttt{TP}_{\texttt{tk}}$ */
  if $L_{i\sqcup} == R_{j\sqcup}$ **then**
    $\texttt{TP}_{\texttt{tk}} \leftarrow \texttt{TP}_{\texttt{tk}} + \text{LEN}(L_i\sqcup)$
  else
    while $L_{i\sqcup}$ and $R_{j\sqcup}$ **do**
      $\texttt{TP}_{\texttt{tk}} \leftarrow \texttt{TP}_{\texttt{tk}} + 1$ **if** $L_{i,i'} == R_{j,j'}$
    end while
  end if
end while
return $\mathcal{C}_{sb}(\mathcal{L}), \mathcal{C}_{tk}(\mathcal{L}), \mathcal{C}_{sb}(\mathcal{R}), \mathcal{C}_{tk}(\mathcal{R})$, $\texttt{TP}_{\texttt{sb}}$, $\texttt{TP}_{\texttt{tk}}$

3.4.3 Examples and Discussion

Figure 3.4 illustrates how the jp-algorithm operates in different scenarios. In the first case, where $L_{\not\sqcup}$ matches $R_{\not\sqcup}$, the algorithm identifies true positive sentence boundaries, denoted by $\texttt{TP}_{\texttt{sb}}$.

The second case presents a condition where no true positive sentence boundary is found initially. In such cases, the algorithm constructs L' and R' by merging adjacent sentences until $L_{\not\sqcup}$ and $R_{\not\sqcup}$ become identical. This merging process constitutes sentence alignment, after which the algorithm can detect true positives among the aligned pairs.

To compute true positives for tokenization, the algorithm compares tokens between L and R. A true positive is counted when $L_i = R_j$, contributing to $\texttt{TP}_{\texttt{tk}}$. Figure 3.5 provides a detailed example showing how the number of true positives for tokens is computed. This step uses the same alignment principle described earlier for sentence-level comparison.

Algorithm 2 JOINT ALGORITHM

function JOINT ALGORITHM ($\mathcal{L}$, $\mathcal{R}$):
Input: $\mathcal{L}$, $\mathcal{R}$
Output: $\mathcal{C}_{sb}(\mathcal{L}), \mathcal{C}_{tk}(\mathcal{L}), \mathcal{C}_{sb}(\mathcal{R}), \mathcal{C}_{tk}(\mathcal{R}), \mathtt{TP_{sb}}, \mathtt{TP_{tk}}$
Obtain $\mathcal{C}_{sb}(\mathcal{L}), \mathcal{C}_{tk}(\mathcal{L})$ from $\mathcal{L}$ and $\mathcal{C}_{sb}(\mathcal{R}), \mathcal{C}_{tk}(\mathcal{R})$ from $\mathcal{R}$
while $\mathcal{L}$ and $\mathcal{R}$ **do**
  /* Obtain $\mathtt{TP_{sb}}$ */
  if $L_{i\not\sqcup} == R_{j\not\sqcup}$ **then**
    $\mathtt{TP_{sb}} \leftarrow \mathtt{TP_{sb}} + 1$
    /* Obtain $\mathtt{TP_{tk}}$ */
    if $L_{i\sqcup} == R_{j\sqcup}$ **then**
      $\mathtt{TP_{tk}} \leftarrow \mathtt{TP_{tk}} + \mathrm{LEN}(L)$
    else
      while $L_{i\sqcup}$ and $R_{j\sqcup}$ **do**
        $\mathtt{TP_{tk}} \leftarrow \mathtt{TP_{tk}} + 1$ **if** $L_{i,i'} == R_{j,j'}$
      end while
    end if
  else
    while $L_{i+1\not\sqcup} \neq R_{j+1\not\sqcup}$ **do**
      $L' \leftarrow L' + L_i$
      $R' \leftarrow R' + R_j$
    end while
    while $L'_{\sqcup}$ and $R'_{\sqcup}$ **do**
      $\mathtt{TP_{tk}} \leftarrow \mathtt{TP_{tk}} + 1$ **if** $L'_{i'} == R'_{j'}$
    end while
  end if
end while
return $\mathcal{C}_{sb}(\mathcal{L}), \mathcal{C}_{tk}(\mathcal{L}), \mathcal{C}_{sb}(\mathcal{R}), \mathcal{C}_{tk}(\mathcal{R}), \mathtt{TP_{sb}}, \mathtt{TP_{tk}}$

	$\mathcal{L}$ (SYSTEM)	$\mathcal{R}$ (GOLD)	
$L_{\not\sqcup} == R_{\not\sqcup}$	`When No. 1 Isn 't the Best ⊓`	`When No. 1 Is n't the Best ⊓`	TP
$L_{\not\sqcup} \neq R_{\not\sqcup}$ (before alignment)	`Mike McConnell 07/06/2000 14:57 John , Hello from South America . ⊓`	`Mike McConnell ⊓` `07/06/2000 14:57 ⊓` `John , Hello from South America . ⊓`	
(after alignment)	`Mike McConnell 07/06/2000 14:57 John , Hello from South America . ⊓`	`Mike McConnell ~~~ 07/06/2000 14:57 ~~~ John , Hello from South America. ⊓`	

Fig. 3.4 Examples illustrating the jp-algorithm from Algorithm 2, showing how true positive sentence boundaries are identified. When boundaries do not initially match, sentence merging is applied

$\mathcal{L}$ (SYSTEM)	When	No.	1	Isn ~~~ 't	the	Best
$\mathcal{R}$ (GOLD)	When	No.	1	Is ~~~ n't	the	Best
	TP	TP	TP	-	TP	TP

Fig. 3.5 Examples illustrating how true positive tokens are identified. When tokens do not initially align, token merging is applied

Length-based sentence alignment algorithms, such as the one described by Gale and Church (1993, p. 83), typically operate under fixed alignment ratios, including 1:0, 0:1, 1:1, 2:1, 1:2, and 2:2. However, in our setting, such fixed-ratio assumptions are insufficient. The system output may segment a single gold sentence into more than two parts, or conversely, a single system sentence may correspond to multiple gold sentences. As a result, sentence boundary mismatches may persist even after applying traditional alignment methods designed for machine translation.

To address this, our algorithm does not rely on predefined alignment types. Instead, we iteratively merge consecutive sentences from L and R until their character sequences match, that is, until $L_{\not\sqcup} = R_{\not\sqcup}$. This merging process replaces fixed-ratio alignment with a flexible mechanism that accommodates arbitrary segmentations.

As implemented in Algorithm 2, when the condition $L_{\not\sqcup} \neq R_{\not\sqcup}$ holds, the algorithm enters the `else` branch to accumulate and merge segments from both L and R until alignment is achieved. This approach supports alignment patterns such as m:1, 1:n, and more generally m:n, allowing it to handle complex sentence segmentation mismatches effectively.

3.5 Case Studies

3.5.1 Case Study on English Corpora

For our case studies, we apply the alignment-based evaluation algorithm to six raw input files from English Universal Dependencies corpora (Nivre et al., 2016, 2020). These include:

1. `GUM`: UD syntax annotations from the Georgetown University Multilayer corpus.
2. `ParTUT`: a multilingual parallel treebank developed at the University of Turin.
3. `EWT`: a gold-standard English UD corpus based on the English Web Treebank.
4. `PUD`: the English portion of the parallel UD treebanks.
5. `LinES`: the English side of the LinES Parallel Treebank.
6. `Pronouns`: a dataset specifically designed for pronoun identification.

We evaluate preprocessing performance using two tools: the `nltk` library (Loper & Bird, 2002; Bird et al.,2009), employing its `word_tokenize` and `sent_tokenize` functions, and the `stanza` toolkit (Qi et al., 2020), which integrates sentence boundary detection and tokenization within its neural pipeline based on Dozat and Manning's biaffine dependency parser (Dozat & Manning, 2017).

Using these tools, we generate preprocessing outputs for each dataset and evaluate them with our alignment-based algorithm. We also compare our results with those obtained from the official CoNLL 2018 Shared Task evaluation script ((Zeman et al., 2018), using `stanza`'s CoNLL-U formatted outputs.[6]

Although both `nltk` and `stanza` perform sentence segmentation and tokenization, they diverge in their treatment of certain edge cases. For example, both tools segment *gift's* into two tokens (*gift* and *'s*) and typically treat final periods as separate tokens. However, `nltk` treats *search-engine* as a single token, whereas `stanza` splits it into three: *search* ␣ - ␣ *engine*. Differences also emerge in sentence segmentation when input lacks clear boundary markers, such as capitalization or terminal punctuation.

Table 3.1 summarizes the evaluation results, including true positives (TP), false positives (FP), and false negatives (FN) for both sentence boundaries and tokens. These are reported for both tools using our alignment-based method, along with the CoNLL evaluation scores applied to `stanza`'s outputs.

The previous evaluation method also employed precision and recall for computing the F1 score, based on counts of true positives (TP), false positives (FP), and false negatives (FN). In the CoNLL 2018 Shared Task evaluation script,[7] both tokens and sentences are treated as spans. When a character-level mismatch occurs in the positions of spans between the system output and the gold file, the script resolves the discrepancy by advancing to the next token in the file with the smaller start offset until the spans align. This procedure is similarly applied to sentence boundaries: the start and end positions of sentence spans are compared between the system and gold data, and a match increments the count of correctly matched sentences (i.e., true positive sentence boundaries).

In contrast, our alignment-based evaluation method restricts this comparison to each aligned sentence pair, ensuring more accurate and localized computation of true positives. Miscounted true positives, especially in preprocessing tasks, can significantly distort evaluation outcomes. Our method directly addresses these issues in the existing evaluation scripts, identifying them as sources of mismatch and proposing adjustments to improve the reliability of sentence preprocessing evaluation.

Nonetheless, due to differences in surface forms, character-level evaluations of preprocessing results from tools like `nltk` and `stanza` may still fail to capture certain divergences. A major contributing factor is the lack of consensus on tokenization conventions across corpora, even within the Universal Dependencies framework. For example, the EWT corpus tokenizes *can't* as *ca* and *n't*, while ParTUT uses *can* and *not*.

We also observe variation in how contractions such as *can't* and *ain't* are represented across corpora. In addition, tools such as `nltk` convert curly quotation marks, including

[6] https://universaldependencies.org/format.html.

[7] https://universaldependencies.org/conll18/conll18_ud_eval.py.

Table 3.1 True positive (TP), false positive (FP), and false negative (FN) counts for sentence boundaries and tokens, evaluated using `nltk` and `stanza`

		GUM			ParTUT			EWT			PUD			LinES			Pronouns		
		TP	FP	FN	TP	FP	FN	TP	FP	FN	TP	FP	FN	TP	FP	FN	TP	FP	FN
SBD	`nltk & jp`	845	137	251	149	2	4	1084	349	993	976	26	24	865	141	170	285	0	0
	`stanza & jp`	1038	38	58	144	6	9	1805	160	272	998	4	2	912	128	123	285	0	0
	`stanza*` & conllu	1038	38	58	144	6	9	1805	160	272	998	4	2	912	128	123	285	0	0
TK	`nltk & jp`	19,443	351	462	3345	27	63	24176	1109	918	20,733	251	443	17,571	56	104	1673	16	32
	`stanza & jp`	19,791	118	114	3381	20	27	24,724	286	370	21,162	18	14	17517	380	158	1649	28	56
	`stanza*` & conllu	19,791	118	114	3381	20	27	24,724	286	370	21,162	18	14	17,517	380	158	1649	28	56

The `stanza` row reports results from the CoNLL-U evaluation script

opening (` `) and closing (' ') quotes, into straight quotes ("), which further contributes to tokenization mismatches.

Since the range of such contractions and symbol conversions is relatively small in English, we compile an exception list to systematically capture these cases. During the final stage of preprocessing evaluation, we cross-check outputs against this list to ensure that the proposed algorithm correctly handles these edge cases.

As a result, the algorithm effectively mitigates the preprocessing mismatches discussed in Sect. 3.3, ensuring that such inconsistencies do not compromise the accuracy of our evaluation procedures.

3.5.2 Case Study on Multilingual Corpora

While our earlier analysis addressed tokenization mismatches involving contractions, additional issues can arise from morphological segmentation, where tokens are split or combined not by mechanical rules but through language-specific analysis. These mismatches are particularly evident in morphologically rich languages, where token boundaries may not correspond directly to whitespace in raw text.

Table 3.2 presents results from case studies on seven GSD treebanks (McDonald et al., 2013) in Universal Dependencies, all provided by Google. For most languages, our alignment-based evaluation yields results consistent with those from the CoNLL UD evaluation script. However, notable divergence is observed in the French GSD corpus.

In the French GSD, multi-word expressions are often tokenized into fewer units than their surface forms suggest. For example, the phrase *de 1 000 mètres* ('of 1000 m') is treated as three tokens in the CoNLL-U data, even though it contains four whitespace-separated units in plain text. This discrepancy does not reflect a shortcoming of our evaluation algorithm, but rather a difference in tokenization conventions between raw text and the linguistically enriched CoNLL-U annotations.

Similar examples can be found in other treebanks. For instance, in `UD_Kurmanji-MG`, a compound verb like *dagir kiriye* ('occupied') is annotated as a single token, despite being written as two separate words. These patterns highlight the need for careful alignment that respects language-specific tokenization practices beyond surface-level segmentation.

3.6 Conclusion

Tokenization and sentence boundary detection are often treated as standardized and reliable components of natural language processing pipelines. Many implementations are reused without further examination, under the assumption that their accuracy is sufficient for most applications. Our investigation shows that when these preprocessing tools are applied to new domains, languages, or formats, they can introduce a non-trivial number of errors,

Table 3.2 True positives (TP), false positives (FP), and false negatives (FN) for sentence boundaries and tokens using `stanza` on multilingual case studies from `UD_*-GSD`, where `*` represents German, Spanish, French, Indonesian, Japanese, Korean, and Portuguese

		DE			ES			FR			ID			JA			KO			PT		
		TP	FP	FN	TP	FP	FN	TP	FP	FN	TP	FP	FN	TP	FP	FN	TP	FP	FN	TP	FP	FN
SBD	`stanza` & `jp`	787	110	190	373	35	53	393	23	23	515	35	42	541	5	2	629	143	360	1161	71	39
	`stanza*` & conllu	787	110	190	373	35	53	393	23	23	515	35	42	541	5	2	629	143	360	1161	71	39
TK	`stanza` & `jp`	16,172	61	52	11,705	33	28	9714	17	22	11,523	9	18	12,750	361	284	11,332	184	345	29,311	52	50
	`stanza*` & conllu	16,172	61	52	11,705	33	28	9710	19	23	11,523	9	18	12,750	361	284	11,332	184	345	29,311	52	50

particularly miscounted true positives, that are rarely examined or reported. These inaccuracies are often buried within intermediate results and therefore remain unnoticed in standard evaluations.

Errors introduced during tokenization or sentence boundary detection do not remain confined to the preprocessing stage. They can propagate through downstream tasks, including dependency parsing, named entity recognition, and machine translation, and can affect both performance and interpretability. Evaluation practices have not addressed the subtleties involved in accurately identifying true positives in sentence and token segmentation.

To address this, we propose an alignment-based evaluation framework grounded in sentence and word alignment principles. This approach explicitly accounts for mismatches between system output and gold references and prevents partial or shifted matches from being incorrectly counted as true positives. The JP-algorithm offers a practical and linguistically informed method for aligning and evaluating sentence and token boundaries with greater precision.

By incorporating alignment into preprocessing evaluation, we provide a more transparent and robust foundation for building end-to-end NLP systems. The results also highlight that segmentation is not merely procedural but reflects deeper assumptions about linguistic structure, and revisiting these assumptions can bring new clarity to model behavior.

Future work may investigate how alignment-based measures operate across typologically diverse languages, where segmentation conventions differ. It may also be fruitful to explore alignment-sensitive objectives that can be incorporated directly into model training, encouraging systems to learn more reliable segmentation strategies. Another direction is to study how segmentation mismatches influence the stability of downstream evaluations, especially in settings where reproducibility is essential.

Through this contribution, we aim to strengthen the foundations of preprocessing evaluation and reaffirm that precision in early stages supports clarity throughout the entire pipeline.

Acknowledgements This chapter is based on "An Untold Story of Preprocessing Task Evaluation: An Alignment-based Joint Evaluation Approach" by Eunkyul Leah Jo, Angela Yoonseo Park, Grace Tianjiao Zhang, Izia Xiaoxiao Wang, Junrui Wang, MingJia Mao, and Jungyeul Park, published in *Proceedings of the 2024 Joint International Conference on Computational Linguistics, Language Resources and Evaluation (LREC-COLING 2024)*, pages 1327–1338, Torino, Italia. ELRA and ICCL (Jo et al., 2024b). An open-source implementation of the tools and resources introduced in this chapter, together with usage examples and documentation, is available at https://github.com/jungyeul/jp-preprocessing.

JP-EVALB

4

4.1 Introduction

Constituency parsing, also known as phrase structure parsing, is a core task in computational linguistics that involves identifying the hierarchical structure of a sentence. The output of a constituency parser is typically a tree that reflects how words group into phrases and how these phrases combine to form larger syntactic units, ultimately capturing the sentence's grammatical organization. This formalism traces back to early generative grammar theories, particularly Chomsky's influential works in the 1950s and 1960s (e.g., Chomsky, 1957, 1965), and has since become foundational in both theoretical linguistics and practical language technologies.

The development of large-scale syntactically annotated corpora, or treebanks (Abeillé, 2003), played a crucial role in enabling data-driven parsing research. Among them, the Penn Treebank (Marcus et al., 1993) has served as a foundational resource for training and evaluating English parsers. Its consistent annotation guidelines and wide adoption facilitated standardized comparisons across models, thereby accelerating progress in both parsing algorithms and evaluation practices. However, these evaluation practices have remained largely unchanged for decades, typically relying on labeled bracketing scores reported in terms of F_1 measures. While such metrics offer a convenient benchmark, they often fail to capture deeper syntactic adequacy or cross-linguistic generalization, issues increasingly central to parsing research.

Evaluating parse trees requires more than verifying correctness at the level of individual decisions; it involves comparing hierarchical structures and constituent spans, a task considerably more intricate than standard classification. As parsing models evolved, from hand-crafted rule-based systems to statistical models and, eventually, neural networks, the need for consistent and meaningful evaluation tools became even more pressing. These tools are expected not only to ensure reproducibility but also to support interpretability in assessing parser quality.

J. Park, *Evaluation by Alignment*, Synthesis Lectures on Computer Science,
https://doi.org/10.1007/978-3-032-16563-3_4

Contemporary neural parsers have dramatically changed the architecture of constituency parsing systems. Rather than explicitly modeling grammar rules, neural parsers typically learn to assign scores to spans of input text, leveraging contextualized word representations. In span-based neural constituency parsing (Kitaev & Klein, 2018; Kitaev et al., 2019), the central idea is to compute a score for every possible span (i, j) in a sentence, potentially labeled with a non-terminal l, using pretrained language models as encoders. These span scores are then composed hierarchically to construct a full parse tree, often through a Cocke–Kasami–Younger (CKY) algorithm (Cocke, 1969; Kasami, 1966; Younger, 1967) like dynamic programming algorithm adapted for neural scoring.

Unlike traditional CKY parsing, which depends on a context-free grammar in Chomsky Normal Form to constrain derivations, neural span-based models dispense with symbolic rules entirely. Instead, they rely on learned representations and scoring functions, typically implemented as multi-layer perceptrons over span encodings, to select the most likely parse. This shift enables models to capture contextual constraints implicitly, such as constituent likelihoods and selectional preferences, without manually defined productions.

The development of neural span-based parsers has led to state-of-the-art results across multiple treebanks. These models combine the expressive power of deep encoders with efficient decoding mechanisms to produce accurate and robust parse trees. While they preserve the core assumption that syntax is compositional and tree structured, they recast parsing as a scoring and search problem over spans, part of a broader trend in NLP to replace explicit linguistic structures with continuous representations learned from data, albeit still guided by the syntactic supervision encoded in annotated corpora.

Alongside span-based approaches, transition-based constituency parsing has seen renewed interest, particularly in models that build non-binary trees directly rather than passing through a binarized representation. These systems diverge from classical shift-reduce parsers by allowing actions that generate arbitrary-arity constituents, thereby better aligning with the structure of human-annotated treebanks. Three notable non-binary transition systems have been proposed: the top-down parser (Dyer et al., 2016), which incrementally predicts constituent labels and their subtrees in a depth-first manner; the in-order parser (Liu & Zhang, 2017), which blends bottom-up evidence with top-down predictions by constructing partial constituents before predicting their parent; and the bottom-up parser (Fernández-González & Gómez-Rodríguez, 2019), which composes subtrees from left to right using a single Reduce action to create arbitrary-arity nodes. All of these systems operate over a stack-buffer configuration and use neural networks to score transition actions, typically employing recurrent or transformer-based encoders to represent the parsing state and capture syntactic context. By removing the need for binarization, these parsers simplify the derivation process and eliminate the overhead of post-processing to recover original tree structures, while maintaining competitive accuracy and decoding speed.

As research on constituency parsing expanded, careful and reproducible evaluation became increasingly important. Parsing does not yield a flat sequence of labels; it produces a hierarchical structure whose correctness depends on how well predicted constituents match the reference in both category and span. This layered comparison is more demanding than in tasks such as tagging or classification, where outputs can be aligned token by token. In constituency parsing, even a small shift in span boundaries can alter the structure of an entire subtree.

To address this need for structural comparison, the field adopted the PARSEVAL evaluation scheme (Black et al., 1991). PARSEVAL introduced a principled way of counting correct constituents by requiring exact matches in their labeled spans. The accompanying tool, EVALB,[1] became the reference implementation and has long provided a shared basis for comparing systems across datasets and modeling approaches.

Within this framework, a predicted constituent is counted as correct only when its label and span correspond exactly to those in the gold-standard tree. These measures, which include labeled precision, labeled recall, and their harmonic mean, have shaped evaluation practice for more than three decades and continue to guide the assessment of both statistical and neural constituency parsers.

Although this framework established a clear standard, EVALB also introduced practical constraints that become visible in modern parsing pipelines. It assumes identical tokenization between the gold file and the system output, enforces a single tree per line, and provides limited error handling when structural mismatches occur. Real-world workflows often violate these assumptions, particularly in multi-stage pipelines where tokenization and sentence segmentation precede parsing. When such mismatches arise, the reported scores can diverge from the true parsing quality.

Following the alignment principles introduced in Chap. 2, this chapter extends the framework to syntactic parsing evaluation. To address these challenges, we introduce an evaluation framework for constituent parsing that refines and extends the original PARSEVAL formulation. Our goal is to make parsing evaluation more robust to the realities of NLP pipelines, where tokenization errors and sentence boundary mismatches are common, and to reduce failure cases that obscure true parser performance. Our new method introduces refined algorithms for computing precision and recall, enabling more accurate and consistent F_1 scores.

We begin this chapter by examining the limitations of current evaluation practices, with particular attention to tokenization mismatches and sentence boundary errors. We then introduce our revised implementation of PARSEVAL metrics, describe the algorithms for resolving mismatch cases, and discuss how they improve upon EVALB. Finally, we provide an extended analysis to demonstrate the reliability, interpretability, and practical value of our evaluation scheme.

This chapter develops a revised framework for evaluating constituency parsing. It begins with a review of the limitations of the standard PARSEVAL scheme and of tools such as EVALB, with particular attention to how assumptions about tokenization, sentence boundaries, and tree formatting influence evaluation outcomes, including previous methods for

[1] The standard EVALB script for labeled precision, recall, and F1 is available at http://nlp.cs.nyu.edu/evalb. The EVALB_SPMRL variant adapts the scoring parameters for multilingual and morphologically rich treebanks (Seddah et al., 2013, 2014).

constituency parsing evaluation (Sect. 4.2). The next section introduces our alignment-based algorithms for parsing evaluation (Sect. 4.3) and explains how they detect and resolve mismatches between system and gold trees, along with examples that illustrate the computation of the revised precision and recall measures. The chapter then examines broader challenges in the evaluation of constituency parsing (Sect. 4.4), including the effects of tokenization mismatches, structural variation across parsers, and difficulties that arise in the context of neural models. This is followed by a series of case studies (Sect. 4.5) that demonstrate how the proposed framework performs on diverse corpora, how it corrects known shortcomings of EVALB, and how it produces more stable and interpretable results than the standard approach. The chapter closes with a discussion of complexity, practical considerations, and implications for future work in syntactic evaluation (Sect. 4.6, Sect. 4.7).

4.2 Limitations of PARSEVAL and Existing Parsing Metrics

To illustrate the motivation behind our new evaluation approach, we first present several known limitations of EVALB that frequently arise in practical settings. One common issue occurs when the terminal nodes of the gold and system trees are not identical, leading to word-level mismatch errors. For instance, the gold tree may contain the token *This*, while the system tree contains *this*. Though semantically equivalent, the evaluation tool treats them as different due to case sensitivity. A simple and effective solution is to normalize all tokens to lowercase, allowing such matches to be treated as equivalent.

A more problematic scenario arises when the gold and system trees differ in their token segmentation. Even when both trees represent the same sentence, differences in preprocessing pipelines such as how contractions, punctuation, or abbreviations are tokenized can cause misalignments at the terminal level. These mismatches are especially frequent with tokens involving periods (e.g., *U.S.*, *Mr.*) or contractions (e.g., *can't*, *won't*), which may be treated as single units or split into multiple tokens depending on the tokenizer. For instance, while one tokenizer may segment *can't* into *ca* and *n't*, another may treat it as the normalized form *cannot*, or expand the contraction into two tokens *can not*. Similarly, sentence-final punctuation can be inconsistently segmented, affecting the alignment between gold and system files.

Under EVALB, such token mismatches prevent the sentence from being evaluated altogether, as the tool requires an exact match between the terminal sequences of both trees. This strict alignment requirement excludes a significant portion of otherwise valid outputs from evaluation. The result is a brittle evaluation procedure, particularly in modern NLP pipelines where preprocessing steps often differ between systems. These cases reveal a major flaw in the standard approach: it cannot compute constituent-level accuracy when tokenization differs, even if the syntactic structure is correct. A more robust evaluation framework should tolerate such surface-level discrepancies and focus on structural correctness in the parse trees.

Example 1:	GOLD	*This ca⊔n't be right⊔.*	
	SYSTEM	*this can⊔not be right⊔.*	where ⊔ *indicates a token delimiter.*

In Example 1, the difference between *ca⊔n't* and *can⊔not*) illustrates a subtle but important source of evaluation error. While a human reader can effortlessly recognize that these token sequences are semantically and syntactically equivalent, `EVALB` does not. Because it requires exact token alignment between the gold and system trees, it treats the entire sentence as invalid for comparison, even when the predicted constituent structure is correct.

Our proposed evaluation approach addresses this limitation by introducing a token-agnostic alignment mechanism. Instead of requiring exact string-level token matches, we allow equivalence classes based on surface normalization or word-level canonicalization. In this case, both (*ca⊔n't*) and (*can⊔not*) generate the same constituent spans and should be treated as equivalent. This adjustment enables more inclusive and realistic assessments of parsing accuracy, especially in settings where preprocessing choices vary across systems.

4.2.1 Methods for Evaluating Parsing Results

Evaluation of constituency parsers has been approached using a variety of metrics, each focusing on different structural aspects of parse trees and handling mismatches in distinct ways. Traditional metrics, such as those implemented in `EVALB`, assume that the gold and predicted trees share an identical sequence of terminal tokens, allowing direct comparison of labeled spans. More recent approaches, including tree alignment and tree edit distance, offer alternative mechanisms that relax or bypass this assumption, enabling evaluation in more realistic scenarios involving tokenization mismatches, segmentation errors, or differing annotation schemes.

To illustrate how different evaluation strategies handle structural and surface-level discrepancies in parse trees, we present in Fig. 4.1 a pair of constituency trees from Example 1: one from a gold-standard annotation and the other from a system's predicted output. Although both trees represent the same underlying sentence, they differ in several important ways. First, the gold tree uses the token *This* with an uppercase initial letter, while the system tree uses *this* in lowercase. Second, the gold tree segments the modal contraction *can't* into two tokens, *ca* and *n't*, while the system tree outputs the full form *can not* as two separate words. For simplicity, the sentence-final punctuation mark has been omitted. Despite these superficial differences, the overall syntactic structures are closely aligned, with identical constituent bracketing beyond the mismatched terminals. As a convention, we include a `TOP` node as the root symbol in both trees, but we do not consider it a constituent for evaluation purposes.

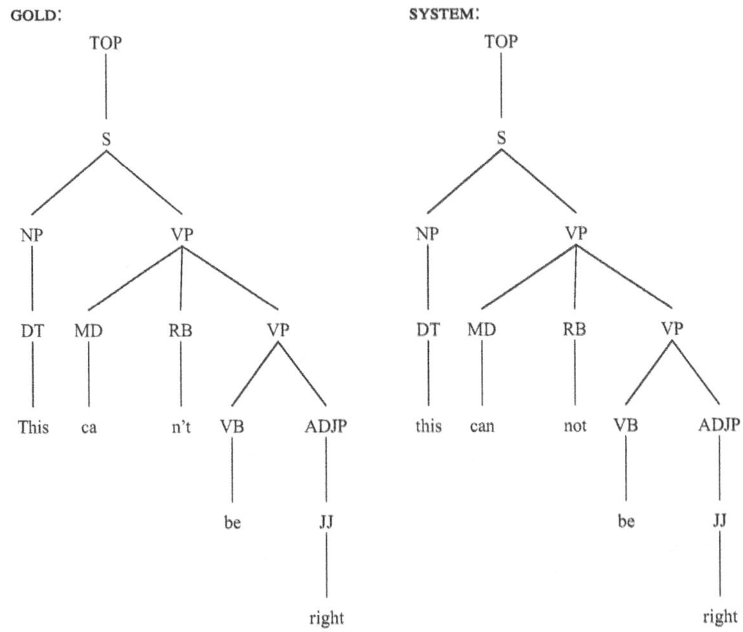

CONSTITUENTS: (S *This ca n't be right*)	(S *this can not be right*)
(NP *This*)	(NP *this*)
(VP *ca n't be right*)	(VP *can not be right*)
(VP *be right*)	(VP *be right*)
(ADJP *right*)	(ADJP *right*)

Fig. 4.1 An illustrative example comparing gold and system parse trees with tokenization and casing differences

This example serves as a concrete test case for understanding how different evaluation metrics interpret such discrepancies. Span-based metrics like EVALB rely on exact token alignment between the gold and predicted trees. In other words, both trees must contain identical sequences of terminal nodes, including the same words, the same letter casing, and the same token boundaries, for any constituent comparison to be performed. In this example, however, the gold tree contains the token *This*, while the system tree has *this*, and the gold sequence *ca* followed by *n't* does not match the system's *can* followed by *not*. Because of these differences, EVALB considers the trees incompatible and excludes the sentence from evaluation.

4.2.1.1 `Aligning Trees`

Earlier work on tree alignment in constituency parsing (Calder, 1997), by contrast, focuses on structural agreement in terms of bracketed spans and may tolerate certain surface-level discrepancies as long as yield alignment remains possible.[2] A notable example is the `aligning trees` approach, which aligns constituency trees from different treebanks for the same sentence, even when part-of-speech tagsets or annotation depths differ. This method identifies aligned subtrees by comparing their terminal yields, that is, the span of tokens each subtree dominates, rather than requiring exact matches of labels or internal structure.

Because the alignment is defined over the sequence of terminal elements, slight textual differences such as casing can be tolerated. For instance, the tokens *This* and *this* may still be aligned if a normalization step maps them to a common form. However, yield alignment fails when token boundaries do not match. In our running example, the gold tree segments *can't* into two tokens, *ca* and *n't*, whereas the system output provides *can* and *not* as separate words. Since the token forms differ, the yields no longer correspond, and alignment between subtrees spanning these tokens is not possible within this framework.

Although the *aligning trees* approach does not return a scalar score like precision or recall, it produces useful quantitative data such as the proportion of aligned terminals or subtrees. These statistics can reveal how consistent two annotation schemes are and where they diverge structurally. As such, the method offers a diagnostic perspective rather than a fully integrated evaluation metric.

To quantify the degree of structural agreement between the gold and system trees in this example, we adopt the alignment coverage measure from the aligning trees framework (Calder, 1997). This metric evaluates the proportion of subtrees in one tree (typically the gold tree) that are structurally aligned with subtrees in another tree (typically the system output). Two subtrees are considered aligned if they share the same terminal yield after terminal alignment is established.

In this case, both the gold and system trees contain five nontrivial subtrees. Among these, three subtrees yield the same span of terminals and can be structurally aligned. These include (1) the noun phrase (NP *This*) aligned with (NP *this*), with the only difference being case, (2) the verb phrase (VP *be right*) aligned with (VP *be right*), and (3) the adjective phrase (ADJP *right*) aligned with (ADJP *right*).

The remaining two subtrees are not aligned due to differences in token segmentation, specifically *ca* + *n't* in the gold tree versus *can* + *not* in the system tree, which cause mismatched yields that prevent subtree alignment.

Following the standard definition, the alignment coverage is computed as:

$$\text{Alignment Coverage} = \frac{\#\ \text{aligned subtrees}}{\#\ \text{total subtrees in the gold tree}} = \frac{3}{5} \tag{4.1}$$

---

[2] This use of the term "alignment" refers specifically to the *aligning trees* method of (Calder, 1997) and should not be confused with the alignment-based evaluation framework introduced later in this chapter.

This result reflects a partial but substantial overlap in structure, despite the presence of tokenization discrepancies that preclude full alignment.

4.2.1.2 Tree Edit Distance

Tree edit distance approaches, such as `tedeval` (Tsarfaty et al., 2012), provide greater flexibility than span-based metrics by allowing for structural comparison between parse trees even when their tokenization or segmentation differs. This is particularly valuable in evaluating parsers for morphologically rich languages, where surface words may correspond to multiple syntactic units after segmentation.

Unlike traditional metrics such as `EVALB`, which require the gold and predicted trees to share the exact sequence of terminal tokens, `tedeval` compares trees based on their structure regardless of surface-level mismatches. It does so by computing the *tree edit distance* (TED) between a predicted tree p and a gold tree g, defined as the minimal number of edit operations required to transform one into the other.

The edit operations considered include adding or deleting:

- Non-terminal nodes labeled with a category c spanning a lattice interval $[i, j]$.
- Terminal nodes represented as lexical entries $\langle s, p \rangle$ with segment s and part of speech p over the same span.

All operations are assigned a unit cost, and only edits that are valid within the morphological segmentation lattice are permitted. This constraint ensures that the evaluation respects the underlying morphological structure of the input.

Given a sequence of edit operations that transforms p into g, the TED score is computed as the sum of operation costs. The final `tedeval` score is then normalized using the following formula:

$$\text{TEDEVAL}(p, g) = 1 - \frac{\text{TED}(p, g)}{|p| + |g| - 2} \tag{4.2}$$

$|p|$ and $|g|$ denote the number of nodes (terminals and non-terminals) in the predicted and gold trees, respectively. In this example, both trees contain 11 nodes, including the `TOP` root.[3] The subtraction of 2 in the denominator accounts for the unpenalized root node (`TOP`) that is common to both trees. The result is a score between 0 and 1, where 1 indicates an exact match and lower scores reflect increasing structural divergence.

Consider a simplified example from Fig. 4.1, where the gold and system trees both parse the sentence *This can't be right*, but differ in surface forms. The gold tree contains the tokens

[3] In `tedeval`, lexical items are not treated as separate labeled nodes. Each token is represented by a single pre-terminal node, that is, its part-of-speech tag, which dominates the lexical string serving as the terminal leaf. Thus, each token contributes one node to the count, represented by its pre-terminal node.

This, ca, n't, while the predicted tree includes *this, can, not*. While the syntactic structure is nearly identical, `tedeval` detects these surface differences as structural mismatches.

Specifically, `tedeval` performs the following operations to transform the predicted tree into the gold tree:

- Delete the terminal node (DT *this*) and insert (DT *This*), because they differ in casing and are treated as distinct lexical items.
- Delete the modal and adverb terminals (MD *can*) and (RB *not*), and insert the corresponding nodes (MD *ca*) and (RB *n't*), reflecting different tokenizations of the contraction *can't*.

These differences result in a total of six edit operations: three deletions and three insertions. The gold tree contains 11 nodes and the predicted tree also contains 11, so the final score is computed as:

$$\text{TEDEVAL}(p, g) = 1 - \frac{6}{11 + 11 - 2} = 1 - \frac{6}{20} = 0.7$$

This score reflects a substantial structural overlap, despite superficial mismatches at the token level. It demonstrates `tedeval`'s capability to assign a graded score even when tokenization, casing, or morphological segmentation differ between the gold and system outputs. Since the score ranges between 0 and 1, with higher values indicating greater structural similarity, `tedeval` enables interpretable, fine-grained comparisons across system outputs.

`tedeval` is robust to token-level inconsistencies and is well suited for evaluating end-to-end systems that jointly perform morphological analysis and syntactic parsing. It provides a single scalar value that quantifies structural similarity, making it both interpretable and comparable across systems and settings. Unlike alignment-based methods that report coverage or agreement statistics, `tedeval` offers a graded, continuous evaluation of structural divergence.

4.2.1.3 EVALB

The standard `EVALB` tool requires the gold and system trees to share an identical sequence of terminal tokens. When the terminal strings differ in casing, token boundaries, or surface forms, the tool cannot establish a one-to-one correspondence between positions in the two trees. As a result, it halts with an error rather than computing labeled precision or recall. In the running example, the gold tree contains *This, ca, n't*, whereas the system tree contains *this, can, not*. Because these sequences do not match exactly, `EVALB` does not evaluate the sentence and reports a token mismatch error.

4.2.2 Summary

The evaluation of syntactic parsers has traditionally relied on metrics that assume exact correspondence between gold and system output at the level of tokenization and sentence boundaries. However, in realistic end-to-end parsing pipelines, mismatches at the word and sentence levels are common, particularly due to differences in tokenization schemes, casing, and sentence segmentation strategies.

Among existing approaches, `EVALB` remains the most widely used metric. It relies on exact span matches between constituent trees, which presupposes perfectly aligned terminal sequences. As a result, even a minor discrepancy in casing or token boundary, such as *This* vs. *this* or *can't* vs. *can not*, can cause an entire sentence to be excluded from evaluation.

More recent approaches have attempted to address structural mismatches using more flexible frameworks. The `aligning trees` method (Calder, 1997) allows subtrees to be aligned based on shared terminal yields, making it possible to identify structurally equivalent constituents even when annotation conventions or token forms differ slightly. However, alignment is still limited to cases where yield spans can be matched, and it does not provide a scalar score for evaluation.

`tedeval` (Tsarfaty et al., 2012) takes this further by defining a tree edit distance between predicted and gold trees, allowing for graded comparisons. It accommodates token-level diferefssnces and segmentation mismatches, making it more suitable for morphologically rich languages or joint segmentation-parsing models. Nevertheless, both `aligning trees` and `tedeval` assume that sentence boundaries between gold and system outputs are already aligned. If a parser splits or merges sentences differently from the reference, such as interpreting *Click here To view it.* as two sentences instead of one, these methods fail to compute evaluation scores at all.

To address this limitation, our proposed method introduces an alignment-driven evaluation procedure that handles mismatches not only at the word level but also across sentence boundaries. By aligning sentences and their constituent spans prior to comparison, the method enables robust evaluation even when preprocessing steps such as sentence splitting or tokenization differ between gold and system outputs. This design makes the approach more realistic for evaluating end-to-end parsers that integrate multiple components, each introducing its own variations.

Table 4.1 summarizes the core characteristics of the discussed methods, focusing on their evaluation mechanism and their ability to accommodate mismatches at different levels of granularity.

Another line of work evaluates constituent parses indirectly by converting them into dependency structures. For example, `sparseval` (Roark et al., 2006) applies a head percolation table (Collins, 1999) to derive head–child relations from constituent trees, allowing

Table 4.1 Comparison to previous parsing evaluation metrics

	Evaluation approach	Addressing mismatches
`aligning trees`	subtree alignment based on yield spans	words
`tedeval`	tree-edit distance based on constituent trees	words
`EVALB`	exact constituent span match	not applicable

standard dependency evaluation metrics to be applied. Likewise, `conllu_eval`[4] (Zeman et al., 2017); (2018), designed for Universal Dependencies and its shared task evaluation, assesses both token and sentence boundaries using span alignment. In this approach, mismatches are handled by advancing through the token sequence until span start positions align, and sentence segmentation is matched by comparing span boundaries.

While these methods are useful in dependency parsing contexts, they still assume consistent sentence-level segmentation or rely on intermediate transformations that abstract away from original constituency structures. In contrast, our proposed method offers a direct and linguistically faithful evaluation of constituency parses, while accommodating both token- and sentence-level variation in end-to-end parsing scenarios.

4.3 Algorithm

Our alignment-based evaluation framework extends the standard PARSEVAL measures by introducing two preprocessing stages, sentence alignment and word alignment, prior to constituent comparison. The goal is to preserve the spirit of PARSEVAL, which evaluates constituent precision, recall, and F1 based on labeled span matches, while relaxing the brittle assumption that gold and system outputs must share identical tokenization and segmentation.

We first introduce the basic notation. Let $\mathcal{T}_\mathcal{L}$ and $\mathcal{T}_\mathcal{R}$ denote the parse trees of the gold and system files, respectively. Each tree dominates a sequence of terminal tokens, written as $\mathcal{L}$ for the gold tree and $\mathcal{R}$ for the system tree. For conciseness, $\mathcal{ST}$ represents the set of all labeled constituents of a tree $\mathcal{T}$, while $C(\mathcal{T})$ is the number of such constituents. A constituent is counted as a true positive when it appears in both sets, i.e., $\mathcal{ST}_\mathcal{L} \cap \mathcal{STR}$. Precision and recall are computed over these counts in the standard manner, but only after alignment has been carried out, as shown in Algorithm 1.

---

[4] The official evaluation script for dependency parsing, used since the *CoNLL 2017 Shared Task on Multilingual Parsing from Raw Text to Universal Dependencies* and updated in 2018, is available at https://universaldependencies.org/conll18/conll18_ud_eval.py.

Algorithm 1 Pseudo-code for new PARSEVAL measures

function PARSEVALMEASURES ($\mathcal{T}_\mathcal{L}$ and $\mathcal{T}_\mathcal{R}$):
  Extract the list of tokens $\mathcal{L}$ and $\mathcal{R}$ from $\mathcal{T}_\mathcal{L}$ and $\mathcal{T}_\mathcal{R}$
  $\mathcal{L}', \mathcal{R}' \leftarrow$ SENTENCEALIGNMENT($\mathcal{L}$, $\mathcal{R}$) where LEN($\mathcal{L}'$) = LEN($\mathcal{R}'$)
  Align trees based on $\mathcal{L}'$ and $\mathcal{R}'$ to obtain $\mathcal{T}_{\mathcal{L}'}$ and $\mathcal{T}_{\mathcal{R}'}$
  while $\mathcal{T}_{\mathcal{L}'}$ and $\mathcal{T}_{\mathcal{R}'}$ **do**
    Extract the list of tokens l and r from $\mathcal{T}_{\mathcal{L}'_i}$ and $\mathcal{T}_{\mathcal{R}'_i}$
    $l', r' \leftarrow$ WORDALIGNMENT(l, r)
    $\mathcal{S}_{\mathcal{T}_\mathcal{L}} \leftarrow$ GETCONSTITUENT($\mathcal{T}_{\mathcal{L}'_i(l')}$, 0) where $0 < i \leq$ LEN($\mathcal{L}'$)
    $\mathcal{S}_{\mathcal{T}_\mathcal{R}} \leftarrow$ GETCONSTITUENT($\mathcal{T}_{\mathcal{R}'_i(r')}$, 0) where $0 < i \leq$ LEN($\mathcal{R}'$)
     $\mathcal{C}(\mathcal{T}_\mathcal{L}) \leftarrow \mathcal{C}(\mathcal{T}_\mathcal{L})+$ LEN($\mathcal{S}_{\mathcal{T}_\mathcal{L}}$)
     $\mathcal{C}(\mathcal{T}_\mathcal{R}) \leftarrow \mathcal{C}(\mathcal{T}_\mathcal{R})+$ LEN($\mathcal{S}_{\mathcal{T}_\mathcal{R}}$)
     while $\mathcal{S}_{\mathcal{T}_\mathcal{L}}$ and $\mathcal{S}_{\mathcal{T}_\mathcal{R}}$ **do**
       if (LABEL, START$_\mathcal{L}$, END$_{\mathcal{L}, l'_j}$) = (LABEL, START$_\mathcal{R}$, END$_{\mathcal{R}, r'_j}$) **then**
         $\mathcal{C}(\texttt{tp}) \leftarrow \mathcal{C}(\texttt{tp}) + 1$
       end if
     end while
   end while
   return $\mathcal{C}(\mathcal{T}_\mathcal{L}), \mathcal{C}(\mathcal{T}_\mathcal{R})$, and $\mathcal{C}(\texttt{tp})$

4.3.1 Stage 1: Sentence Alignment

The first stage reconciles differences in sentence segmentation. Even when gold and system outputs are based on the same raw text, they may differ in how sentences are delimited, for example when one tokenizer merges two clauses into a single sentence while the other splits them. To handle this, we accumulate adjacent sentences on each side until a matching pair can be identified, effectively re-indexing the trees into aligned pairs $\mathcal{T}_{\mathcal{L}'}$ and $\mathcal{T}_{\mathcal{R}'}$. In practice, sentence boundaries are ignored during alignment and reinstated only once equivalence is achieved. We introduce the notation $\not\sqcup$ to indicate spaces removed during alignment, ensuring that mismatches due to punctuation or tokenization conventions do not hinder the procedure. The full algorithm is provided in Algorithm 2.

Algorithm 2 Pseudo-code for sentence alignment

function SENTENCEALIGNMENT ($\mathcal{L}$, $\mathcal{R}$):
  while $\mathcal{L}$ and $\mathcal{R}$ **do**
    if $(\mathcal{L}_{i(\not\sqcup)} = \mathcal{R}_{j(\not\sqcup)})$ ▷ CASE 1 $_{(i,j)}$
      $\vee (\mathcal{L}_{i(\not\sqcup)} \simeq \mathcal{R}_{j(\not\sqcup)} \wedge (\mathcal{L}_{i+1(\not\sqcup)} = \mathcal{R}_{j+1(\not\sqcup)} \vee \mathcal{L}_{i+1(\not\sqcup)} \simeq \mathcal{R}_{j+1(\not\sqcup)}))$ ▷ CASE 2 $_{(i,j)}$
    then
      $\mathcal{L}', \mathcal{R}' \leftarrow \mathcal{L}' + \mathcal{L}_i, \mathcal{R}' + \mathcal{R}_j$ where $0 < i \leq \text{LEN}(\mathcal{L}), 0 < j \leq \text{LEN}(\mathcal{R})$
    else
      while $\neg$(CASE 1 $_{(i+1,j+1)} \vee$ CASE 2 $_{(i+1,j+1)}$) **do**
        if $\text{LEN}(\mathcal{L}_i) < \text{LEN}(\mathcal{R}_j)$ **then**
          $L' \leftarrow L' + \mathcal{L}_i$
          $i \leftarrow i + 1$
        else
          $R' \leftarrow R' + \mathcal{R}_j$
          $j \leftarrow j + 1$
        end if
      end while
      $\mathcal{L}', \mathcal{R}' \leftarrow \mathcal{L}' + L', \mathcal{R}' + R'$
    end if
  end while
  return $\mathcal{L}', \mathcal{R}'$

4.3.2 Stage 2: Word Alignment

Within each aligned sentence pair, word-level mismatches are resolved. Tokenization differences, such as *ca+n't* versus *can+not* or casing differences like *This* versus *this*, are common sources of failure in standard EVALB. Our method accumulates unmatched tokens into buffers until the next pairwise match is found, thereby aligning subsequences of tokens between gold and system sentences. This strategy is lightweight, relying on pattern matching rather than probabilistic inference, which suffices under the assumption that the two sides represent the same underlying sentence. The full algorithm is given in Algorithm 3.

4.3.3 Stage 3: Constituent Extraction and Comparison

Once sentence and word alignments are established, we extract constituents from the aligned trees. Each constituent is represented as a tuple (LABEL, START, END, YIELD), recording its category, span indices, and terminal yield. The sets of constituents are then compared: for every gold constituent, we check whether an identical label-span pair exists in the system output. True positives are incremented accordingly, and precision, recall, and F1 are then computed in the usual PARSEVAL manner. The full algorithm is given in Algorithm 4.

Algorithm 3 Pseudo-code for word alignment

```
function WORDALIGNMENT (l, r):
  while l and r do
    if (l_i = r_j)                                    ▷ CASE 1 (i,j)
       ∨ ((l_i ≠ r_j) ∧ (l_{i+1} = r_{j+1}))          ▷ CASE 2 (i,j)
     then
      l', r' ← l_i, r_j where 0 < i ≤ LEN(l), 0 < j ≤ LEN(r)
    else
      while ¬(CASE 1 (i+1,j+1) ∨ CASE 2 (i+1,j+1)) do
        if (LEN(l) − LEN(l_0, l_i)) > (LEN(r) − LEN(r_0, r_j)) then
          ll ← ll + l_i
          i ← i + 1
        else
          rr ← rr + r_j
          j ← j + 1
        end if
      end while
      l', r' ← ll, rr
    end if
  end while
  return l', r'
```

Algorithm 4 Pseudo-code for getting constituents

```
function GETCONSTITUENT (𝒯, start):
  if HEIGHT(𝒯)>2 then
    END ← START + LEN(LEAVES(𝒯))
    𝒮_𝒯 ← 𝒮_𝒯 + (LABEL(𝒯), START, END, LEAVES(𝒯))
    while T do
      GETCONSTITUENT(𝒯_i, start) where 𝒯_i is a child of 𝒯
      START ← LEN(LEAVES(𝒯_i))
    end while
  end if
  return 𝒮_𝒯
```

4.3.4 Design Considerations

This algorithm is deliberately simpler than alignment methods used in bilingual machine translation, where recursive editing and expectation–maximization are often required due to fundamental differences between languages. In our case, gold and system trees are monolingual and differ only in surface tokenization or sentence boundaries. By restricting ourselves to pattern-based accumulation and direct matching, we achieve robustness without introducing unnecessary complexity.

4.3.5 Summary

In essence, our algorithm can be viewed as a thin alignment layer wrapped around the standard PARSEVAL scoring scheme. By resolving segmentation mismatches before constituent comparison, it ensures that evaluation reflects true structural agreement rather than artefacts of preprocessing. This design allows us to retain the interpretability and continuity of PARSEVAL while making it applicable to end-to-end parsing systems that integrate tokenization and sentence segmentation.

4.4 Handling Mismatches in Constituency Parsing Evaluation

4.4.1 Word Mismatch

We have observed that the expression of contractions varies significantly, resulting in inherent challenges related to word mismatches. As the number of contractions and symbols to be converted in a language is finite, we composed an exception list for our system to capture such cases for each language and thereby facilitate the word alignment process between gold and system sentences. In the following example, we achieve perfect precision and recall of 5/5 for both because their constituent trees are exactly matched, regardless of any mismatched words.

			(GOLD)					(SYSTEM)			
$S_{(0,4)}$			$NP_{(0,1)}$	DT	^{0}*This*	^{0}*this*	DT	$NP_{(0,1)}$			$S_{(0,4)}$
	$VP_{(1,4)}$			MD	$^{1.0}$*ca*	$^{1.0}$*can*	MD			$VP_{(1,4)}$	
				RB	$^{1.1}$*n't*	$^{1.1}$*not*	RB				
		$VP_{(2,4)}$		VB	^{2}*be*	^{2}*be*	VB		$VP_{(2,4)}$		
			$AdjP_{(3,4)}$	JJ	^{3}*right*	^{3}*right*	JJ	$AdjP_{(3,4)}$			

This case illustrates one of the simplest and most frequent forms of mismatch: superficial variation in tokenization or casing. Although the gold tree uses the contraction *ca+n't* and the system tree expands it as *can+not*, both analyses produce structurally identical constituent spans. Under EVALB, the sentence would be discarded due to non-identical terminals; under our framework, word alignment pairs $^{1.0}$*ca*, $^{1.1}$*n't* with $^{1.0}$*can*, $^{1.1}$*not*, allowing evaluation to proceed. This example shows that word-level normalization or alignment prevents tokenization artefacts from obscuring genuine structural agreement.[5]

---

[5] The current pattern-based word alignment procedure in the JP- FRAMEWORK aligns the pairs *ca, n't* and *can not* by treating them as equivalent multi-token expressions. Other alignment algorithms may

GOLD	^{0}*This*	$^{1.0}$*ca*	$^{1.1}$*n't*	^{2}*be*	^{3}*right*
SYSTEM	^{0}*this*	$^{1.0}$*can*	$^{1.1}$*not*	^{2}*be*	^{3}*right*

The effectiveness of the word alignment approach remains intact even when mismatches are more substantial, such as in morphologically rich languages where "morphological segmentation is not the inverse of concatenation" (Tsarfaty et al., 2012). In these cases, token boundaries may not simply differ in surface form but instead reflect distinct analyses of morphological fusion or splitting. We illustrate this with an example in Hebrew from Tsarfaty et al. (2012), where determiners and adjectives appear either as separate morphemes or as fused tokens depending on the tokenizer.

GOLD	^{0}*B*	$^{1.0}$*H*	$^{1.1}$*CL*	^{2}*FL*	^{3}*HM*	$^{4.0}$*H*	$^{4.1}$*NEIM*
	'in'	'the'	'shadow'	'of'	'them'	'the'	'pleasant'
SYSTEM	^{0}*B*	^{1}*CL*		^{2}*FL*	^{3}*HM*	^{4}*HNEIM*	
	'in'	'shadow'		'of'	'them'	'made-pleasant'	

In this example, the gold tree represents the noun phrase the shadow' as two morphemes (*H* + *CL*), while the system tree treats it as a single token (*CL*). Similarly, the adjective phrase the pleasant' is represented in the gold tree as two morphemes but in the system tree as the fused form *HNEIM* 'made-pleasant'. Despite these differences, the alignment procedure merges or splits tokens until they are reconciled, aligning $^{1.0}H$, $^{1.1}CL$ with ^{1}CL, and $^{4.0}H$, $^{4.1}NEIM$ with $^{4}HNEIM$. This alignment results in a precision of 4/4 and recall of 4/6, capturing the majority of structurally equivalent constituents even though the surface analyses differ.

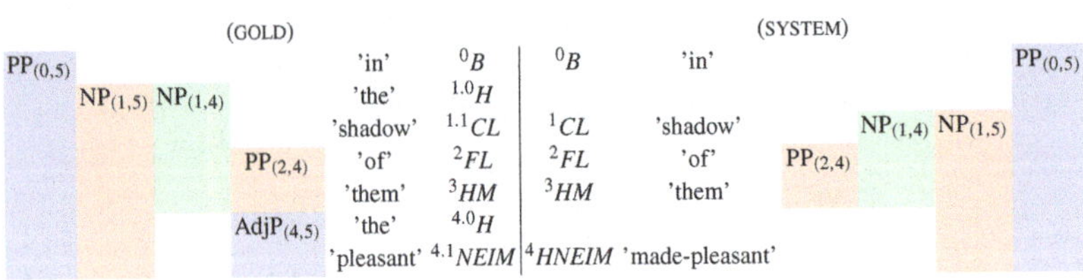

These examples demonstrate the range of mismatches addressed by our method. At one end are surface-level issues such as case normalization and contractions, while at the other are deeper morphological variations where token boundaries reflect different analyses of the same linguistic unit. In both scenarios, alignment-based evaluation allows constituent structures to be compared fairly, preventing spurious mismatches from artificially lowering parsing accuracy.

---

instead align *ca* with *can* and *n't* with *not* as separate pairs, depending on their token-level matching strategy.

4.4.2 Sentence Mismatch

Sentence mismatches arise when the gold and system outputs differ in their segmentation or boundary decisions, producing distinct root structures. Rather than discarding such cases, we merge the trees under a dummy root node, for example @S, which serves as a pseudo root for merging sentences and is ignored during evaluation. This strategy allows comparison of internal constituents while preserving the structural divergence at the root level.

In the following example, the gold parse spans the sentence as $S_{(0,6)}$, while the system parse introduces an additional segmentation, producing $S_{(0,5)}$ and $S_{(2,6)}$. By merging the two trees under @S, we retain both analyses in a single alignment space. This procedure results in a precision of 5/8 and a recall of 5/7.

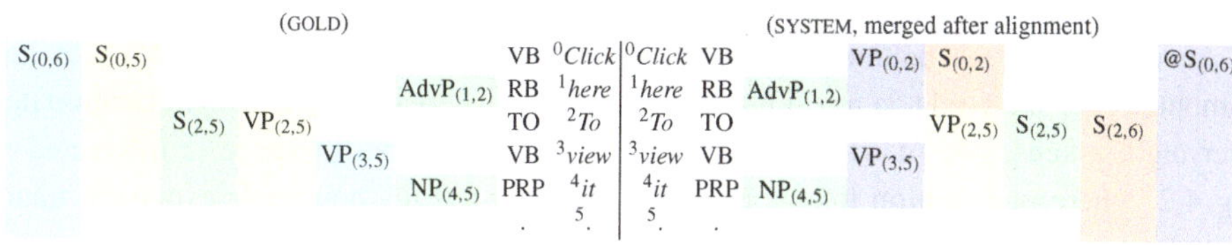

This example illustrates how our framework treats mismatches that cannot be resolved by local token alignment alone. Even when sentences differ in their root segmentation, aligning them under a dummy node makes it possible to evaluate shared internal structures fairly. In this way, our method ensures that errors in sentence boundary decisions do not completely obscure the recognition of correctly parsed constituents within the sentence.

4.4.3 Assumptions

To handle discrepancies in morphological analysis that arise in parse trees during evaluation, we introduce two guiding assumptions.

(i) A full-tree constituent is counted as a true positive if the gold and system sentences are aligned and their root labels match, even when the internal morphological segmentation or analysis differs. This assumption reflects the idea that differences in how words are segmented morphologically should not affect the recognition of structural equivalence at the sentence level, provided that both trees correspond to the same underlying sentence.

(ii) A subtree constituent is counted as a true positive if its lexical items align through word alignment and its phrase labels are identical in both trees. This assumption ensures that smaller syntactic units are still credited when they are structurally equivalent, even if surrounding morphology diverges between the two analyses.

This assumption ensures that smaller syntactic units are still credited when they are structurally equivalent, even if surrounding morphology diverges between the two analyses.

4.5 Case Studies

4.5.1 Dealing with Punctuation Marks

Punctuation marks present a subtle but important challenge in evaluation. The original EVALB treats punctuation as extraneous and excludes problematic symbols from the constituent list. In contrast, JP- EVALB includes all tokens that appear in the sentence, ensuring that bracket indices and word counts reflect the complete sequence of tokens in both the gold and system parse trees.

Accuracy in the last column of the result is therefore defined differently: in EVALB, it is computed over six word tokens excluding punctuation, whereas in JP- EVALB, it is computed over eight tokens, two of which are punctuation marks. This difference is illustrated in Fig. 4.2, where punctuation tokens are highlighted in red to show their exclusion under EVALB.

The inclusion of punctuation in JP- EVALB does not alter the overall count of constituents, since punctuation marks do not form constituents on their own. However, it ensures that part-of-speech tagging accuracy is evaluated against the full sentence, including punctuation, and that word alignment between gold and system sentences is not distorted by excluded symbols. This distinction becomes particularly relevant in multilingual settings where punctuation conventions vary (e.g., quotation marks in East Asian scripts or spacing rules in French), and consistency in evaluation requires treating punctuation as part of the input.

4.5.2 Section 23 of the English Penn Treebank

We benchmarked our implementation on Section 23 of the English Penn Treebank, the standard test set for English constituency parsing. Under identical conditions where sentences and words match exactly, the proposed method requires approximately 4.5 s to evaluate the full section. On the same machine, EVALB completes the task in less than 0.1 s.

This substantial difference in runtime is expected and reflects two factors. First, EVALB is implemented in C, a compiled language optimized for speed, whereas our current implementation is written in Python, an interpreted language with slower execution. Second, our approach introduces additional alignment stages at both the sentence and word levels. These steps ensure that mismatches in tokenization, contractions, or sentence boundaries are handled robustly, but they incur overhead that EVALB does not face.

Despite these runtime differences, the evaluation outputs of the two systems are largely comparable. Figure 4.3 presents excerpts from three result files generated by EVALB and by

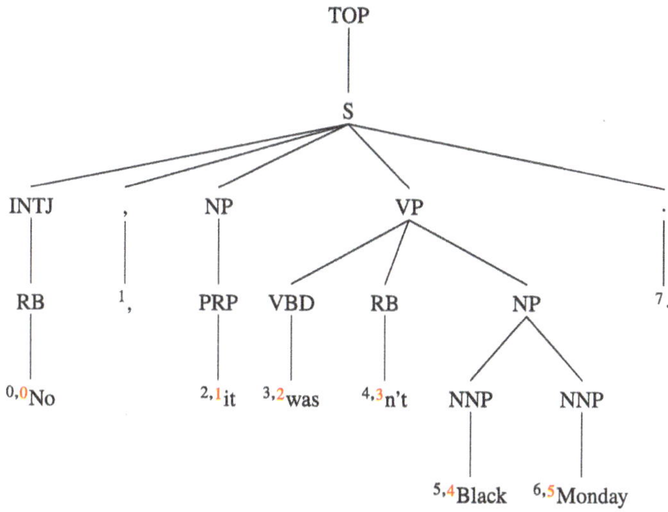

(a) Example of the parse tree

```
('S', 0, 8, "No , it was n't Black Monday .")
('INTJ', 0, 1, 'No')
('NP', 2, 3, 'it')
('VP', 3, 7, "was n't Black Monday")
('NP', 5, 7, 'Black Monday')
```

(b) List of constituents by JP-EVALB

```
('S', 0, 6, "No it was n't Black Monday")
('INTJ', 0, 1, "No")
('NP', 1, 2, "it")
('VP', 2, 6, "was n't Black Monday")
('NP', 4, 6, "Black Monday")
```

(c) List of constituents by EVALB

Fig. 4.2 Difference between JP- EVALB and EVALB

our proposed method, using parse trees produced by the PCFG-LA Berkeley parser (Petrov and Klein, 2007). As discussed in Sect. 4.2, the results may differ slightly because EVALB excludes constituents containing certain symbols or punctuation marks, while JP- EVALB evaluates over the complete set of tokens. These differences can lead to small variations in precision, recall, or tagging accuracy, but the overall evaluation trends remain consistent.

Finally, we note that JP- EVALB can reproduce the exact output of EVALB when required. This "legacy mode" ensures backward compatibility for researchers who wish to compare results directly with earlier work while still benefiting from the enhanced alignment features of our implementation.

```
Sent                          Mt  Br  Cr   Co    Tag
ID  L St      Re        Pr Br gd te Br Wd Tg     Acc
----------------------------------------------------
 1  8  0 100.00 100.00   5  5  5  0  8  7  87.50
 2 40  0  70.97  73.33 22 31 30  7 40 40 100.00
 3 31  0  95.24  95.24 20 21 21  0 31 31 100.00
 4 35  0  90.48  86.36 19 21 22  2 35 35 100.00
 5 26  0  86.96  86.96 20 23 23  2 26 25  96.15
.....
```

(a) Example of JP-EVALB results considering punctuation marks during evaluation

```
Sent                          Mt  Br  Cr   Co    Tag
ID  L St      Re        Pr Br gd te Br Wd Tg     Acc
----------------------------------------------------
 1  8  0 100.00 100.00   5  5  5  0  6  5  83.33
 2 40  0  70.97  73.33 22 31 30  7 37 37 100.00
 3 31  0  95.24  95.24 20 21 21  0 26 26 100.00
 4 35  0  90.48  86.36 19 21 22  2 32 32 100.00
 5 26  0  86.96  86.96 20 23 23  2 24 23  95.83
.....
```

(b) Example of JP-EVALB results with the legacy option, which produces the exact same results as EVALB

```
Sent                          Mt  Br  Cr   Co    Tag
ID  L St      Re        Pr Br gd te Br Wd Tg     Acc
----------------------------------------------------
 1  8  0 100.00 100.00   5  5  5  0  6  5  83.33
 2 40  0  70.97  73.33 22 31 30  7 37 37 100.00
 3 31  0  95.24  95.24 20 21 21  0 26 26 100.00
 4 35  0  90.48  86.36 19 21 22  2 32 32 100.00
 5 26  0  86.96  86.96 20 23 23  2 24 23  95.83
.....
```

(c) Example of the original EVALB results

Fig. 4.3 Examples of evaluation results on Section 23 of the English Penn treebank

Fig. 4.4 Evaluation results of bug cases

```
Sent                       Mt  Br  Cr   Co    Tag
ID  L St    Re     Pr   Br gd te Br Wd Tg    Acc
-------------------------------------------------
 1 37  0 77.27 62.96 17 22 27  5 37 30 81.08
 2 21  0 69.23 60.00  9 13 15  2 21 17 80.95
 3 47  0 77.78 80.00 28 36 35  4 48 43 89.58
 4 26  0 33.33 35.29  6 18 17  8 27 19 70.37
 5 44  0 42.31 32.35 11 26 34 17 44 33 75.00
```

4.5.3 Bug Cases Identified by EVALB

We next examined the well-known bug cases documented in EVALB. Figure 4.4 illustrates all five cases and shows that our proposed implementation successfully evaluates them without failures.

In three of the cases (sentences 1, 2, and 5), the issue arises because certain symbols are treated as words during POS tagging. This treatment causes a mismatch in sentence length: while the gold parse tree includes these symbols as tokens, EVALB discards them during evaluation, leading to discrepancies in word counts. Our approach resolves this by not disregarding any labels or symbols, instead including them as words in the evaluation. Consequently, POS tagging accuracy in our framework is based on the complete token sequence, ensuring consistency between gold and system trees. By contrast, `EVALB` reports POS accuracy relative only to words, excluding symbols.

The remaining two cases (sentences 3 and 4) involve genuine word mismatches where trace symbols (*-*num*) are inserted in the trees. Since these insertions alter the tokenization, `EVALB` fails to align the sentences and cannot compute scores. Our algorithm, however, overcomes this limitation by applying sentence alignment followed by word alignment, allowing mismatched tokens to be reconciled before constituent comparison.

These bug cases illustrate a central strength of our approach: by handling punctuation, symbols, and trace insertions systematically, our method ensures that evaluation can proceed even in situations where `EVALB` fails or produces inconsistent results.

This robustness makes the framework more suitable for cross-linguistic or morphologically complex treebanks where such discrepancies are frequent.

4.5.4 Korean End-to-End Parsing Evaluation

We further evaluated our framework on Korean, conducting an end-to-end experiment in which system-segmented sequences served as the input for constituency parsing. Unlike in English, these sequences frequently diverge from their corresponding gold-standard sentences and tokens due to differences in sentence boundary detection and morphological segmentation.

To simulate this pipeline, we combined the following resources: (i) A test set of 148 sentences (comprising 4538 morphemes) from `BGAA0001` of the Korean Sejong treebank, as described in Kim and Park (2022). For this experiment, the sentences were concatenated into a single text block. (ii) POS tagging and morpheme segmentation produced by `sjmorph.model` (Park and Tyers, 2019), a morphological analyzer whose pipeline also performs sentence boundary detection and tokenization.[6] This output constitutes the parser's input format. (iii) A Korean Berkeley parser model trained on the Sejong treebank (Park et al., 2016).[7]

Figure 4.5 presents a showcase of the resulting end-to-end constituency parsing evaluation. The pipeline naturally introduces both sentence mismatches (when system and gold boundaries differ) and word mismatches (when morpheme segmentations diverge). As a result, the system output consisted of 123 sentences and 4367 morphemes, compared to 148 sentences and 4538 morphemes in the gold data.

Despite these discrepancies, JP- EVALB successfully aligned the system and gold parses through its two-step alignment strategy. Once alignment was established, the evaluation pro-

[6] https://github.com/jungyeul/sjmorph.

[7] https://zenodo.org/records/3995084.

```
Sent                    Mt  Br  Cr     Co   Tag
ID  L St    Re      Pr Br gd te Br Wd Tg    Acc
-----------------------------------------------
 1 28  0 85.71 85.71 18 21 21  3 29 26 89.66
 2 27  0 91.30 84.00 21 23 25  2 28 25 89.29
 3 33  0 88.00 88.00 22 25 25  3 35 31 88.57
 4 43  0 72.73 72.73 24 33 33  7 43 40 93.02
 5 18  0 69.57 84.21 16 23 19  2 19 12 63.16
.....
```

Fig. 4.5 Evaluation results of the end-to-end Korean constituency parsing

ceeded as usual, yielding valid scores even in the presence of segmentation and boundary differences. This demonstrates that JP-EVALB can handle real-world scenarios of Korean parsing where tokenization and sentence boundaries are inherently unstable, extending evaluation capabilities beyond the assumptions built into EVALB.

4.6 Discussion

4.6.1 Complexity

The proposed algorithm preserves linear-time complexity. Sentence and word alignment is computed in $O(I + J)$ time, where I and J denote the lengths (in tokens) of the gold and system sentences, respectively. Constituent matching is performed by a tree traversal procedure with complexity $O(N + E)$, where N is the number of nodes and E is the number of edges in the constituent trees.

Hence, the overall runtime is

$$O(I + J + N + E),$$

which remains linear in the size of the input. This matches the asymptotic complexity of the original EVALB, with the only additional cost being the alignment-based preprocessing step required to reconcile sentence and word mismatches.

In the *worst case*, when every sentence or word requires alignment, the additional $O(I + J)$ step is fully incurred. In the *average case*, however, mismatches are relatively rare, and alignment either reduces to near-constant overhead or is amortized across the corpus. As a result, the runtime behavior in practice is dominated by the $O(N + E)$ traversal cost, making the proposed algorithm nearly indistinguishable from EVALB in terms of efficiency while providing strictly broader coverage.

4.6.2 A Note on Constituent Parsing

Syntactic analysis in current language technology is predominantly carried out with dependency representations, which also underpin much of higher-level semantic parsing. Dependency parsing and its evaluation offer clear advantages: grammatical relations are represented directly and parsing algorithms are often simpler and more efficient.

Constituent parsing by contrast preserves the full hierarchical structure of sentences. This hierarchical information is valuable for modeling phrase organization and their interactions, and remains central to many theories of formal syntax. Research in combinatory categorial grammar parsing (Lewis et al., 2016; Lee et al., 2016; Stanojević & Steedman, 2020; Yamaki et al., 2023) and tree-adjoining grammar (TAG) parsing (Kasai et al., 2017, 2018) illustrates that these constituent-based frameworks often embed dependency structures within richer derivational formalisms.

Beyond these grammar-based approaches, novel methods such as linearization-based constituency parsing (Vinyals et al., 2015; Fernández-González & Gómez-Rodríguez, 2020; Wei et al., 2020) have demonstrated that constituent structures can be learned effectively in neural models.

If an end-to-end system is to exploit constituent representations, however, the evaluation methodology must be robust enough to assess the correctness of hierarchical structure, not merely dependency edges. This is precisely the motivation for extending evaluation beyond the scope of EVALB.

4.7 Conclusion

Despite the widespread use and acceptance of the previous implementation of PARSEVAL measures as the *de facto* standard for constituency parsing evaluation, it suffers from a significant limitation: the requirement of task-specific, highly constrained input conditions. In practice, real-world parsing pipelines are subject to mismatches introduced during earlier steps such as sentence boundary detection, tokenization, or morphological segmentation. When such discrepancies occur, the original EVALB either fails or produces misleading results, limiting its applicability in modern end-to-end parsing systems.

Numerous alternatives have been proposed to alleviate these issues, often by introducing complex tree transformations or by shifting toward dependency-based scoring metrics. While such methods offer valuable perspectives, they depart from the core PARSEVAL framework, complicating direct comparability with decades of prior research.

Our proposed JP- EVALB framework takes a different approach. By introducing sentence and word alignment as a lightweight preprocessing step, it resolves the mismatch problem without modifying the underlying PARSEVAL definitions. This preserves both the interpretability and the mathematical simplicity of the original measures while extending their applicability to noisy or imperfectly aligned input. Formally, the alignment step runs in linear time, ensuring that the overall computational complexity remains unchanged from the original EVALB. In practice, this means that the rich body of prior work evaluated with PARSEVAL remains directly comparable to evaluations performed with JP- EVALB.

Beyond backward compatibility, JP- EVALB opens new possibilities. It enables meaningful evaluation of constituent parsers in fully end-to-end settings, where preprocessing modules (sentence segmentation, tokenization, morphological analysis) may introduce discrepancies with gold-standard annotations. It also provides robustness across languages, as demonstrated by our Korean evaluation experiments, where mismatches are common due to the intricacies of morphological segmentation. In addition, the system successfully handles known bug cases in EVALB and integrates punctuation consistently, further strengthening its reliability.

In summary, JP- EVALB can be viewed not only as a replacement for the original EVALB but as a bridge between older practices and current needs. It maintains compatibility with the established PARSEVAL tradition while extending its scope to the realities of modern parsing research. We believe this framework provides a foundation for more comprehensive and linguistically faithful evaluation of constituent parsing, and we anticipate its adoption will support both continuity with past work and innovation in future end-to-end parsing systems.

Acknowledgements This chapter is based on (i) "A Novel Alignment-based Approach for PARSEVAL Measures" by Eunkyul Leah Jo, Angela Yoonseo Park, and Jungyeul Park, published in *Computational Linguistics* (Jo et al., 2024a), and (ii) "JP- EVALB: Robust Alignment-based PARSEVAL Measures" by Jungyeul Park, Junrui Wang, Eunkyul Jo, Angela Park, published in *Proceedings of the 2024 Conference of the North American Chapter of the Association for Computational Linguistics: Human Language Technologies (Volume 3: System Demonstrations)*, pages 70âŁ"77, Mexico City, Mexico (Park et al., 2024). An open-source implementation of the alignment-based PARSEVAL framework, including detailed usage instructions and reproducible results for all case studies presented in §4.5, is available at https://github.com/jungyeul/alignment-based-PARSEVAL.

JP-ERRANT

5

5.1 Introduction

Grammatical error correction (GEC) is a core task in natural language processing that focuses on the automatic identification and correction of grammatical errors in written text (Bryant et al., 2023). It is particularly relevant in second language acquisition, where learner outputs frequently diverge from standard grammatical norms due to transfer effects, limited exposure, or incomplete mastery of morphosyntactic rules. GEC is typically formulated as a monolingual sequence-to-sequence generation task: given an input sentence containing errors, the system produces a revised sentence that retains the intended meaning while improving grammaticality, fluency, and coherence. The task requires addressing a wide range of error types, including agreement mismatches, tense inconsistencies, preposition and article misuse, word order errors, and subtler issues of register or style.

The development of GEC has advanced alongside broader progress in NLP. Early systems used rule-based methods or statistical classifiers trained on annotated learner corpora, but these approaches were limited by narrow coverage and poor generalizability. The field gained momentum with the adoption of statistical machine translation, which framed GEC as monolingual translation from ungrammatical to corrected text. Neural models, especially encoder–decoder architectures with attention mechanisms and, later, transformer-based pretrained models, have further improved correction accuracy by capturing long-range dependencies and producing more fluent output.

The recent emergence of large-scale pretrained generative language models, especially those fine-tuned for instruction following, has transformed approaches to GEC. Rather than relying solely on fine-tuned neural models trained on parallel learner corpora, as in earlier work, prompting-based GEC has gained increasing traction, wherein general-purpose language models are guided to perform correction through carefully designed textual prompts. This shift reflects a broader trend in NLP toward task generalization and few-shot learning,

J. Park, *Evaluation by Alignment*, Synthesis Lectures on Computer Science,
https://doi.org/10.1007/978-3-032-16563-3_5

where correction capability emerges from pretrained knowledge rather than task-specific optimization.

Prompting-based GEC enables models to correct grammatical errors without extensive retraining, often achieving competitive performance compared to supervised baselines, particularly in high-resource languages (Zeng et al., 2024). Moreover, prompting frameworks allow for flexible error correction behavior, such as controlling conservativeness, preserving learner style, or targeting specific error types, simply by modifying the instruction. This approach also facilitates multilingual and cross-lingual correction, as the underlying model can leverage its exposure to diverse linguistic structures during pretraining.

In practical terms, GEC serves a dual purpose: it functions both as an assistive technology for learners and as a foundational component in intelligent language learning environments. For language learners, GEC systems offer immediate, automated feedback that fosters metalinguistic awareness and facilitates the internalization of target language norms. For instructors, such systems alleviate the repetitive burden of manual error correction and annotation, allowing them to focus on more targeted and effective pedagogical interventions. Beyond the classroom, GEC is also embedded in writing support tools for both native and non-native speakers, improving the grammatical quality of formal communication across academic, professional, and social contexts. Yet, despite its pedagogical and applied value, evaluating GEC output remains conceptually challenging.

Unlike purely discriminative tasks such as part-of-speech tagging or syntactic parsing, GEC operates under conditions of *correctional multiplicity*: there are often many plausible ways to revise an erroneous sentence. For instance, a learner sentence like *She give me a book* can be corrected as either *She gives me a book* or *She gave me a book*, depending on the intended tense.[1]

---

[1] This flexibility is captured by the M2 annotation format, which allows multiple corrections from different annotators to be recorded for the same span, and whose format we will describe later in this chapter:

```
S She give me a book
A 1 2|||R:VERB:SVA|||gives|||REQUIRED|||-NONE-|||0
A 1 2|||R:VERB:TENSE|||gave|||REQUIRED|||-NONE-|||1
```

In the above M2 annotation format, each sentence begins with the letter `S` (source) followed by the original learner sentence. Here, the tokens are indexed from zero, so `0` corresponds to *She*, `1` to *give*, and so on. Each grammatical edit is described in an annotation line beginning with `A` (annotation), followed by the start and end token indices of the erroneous span, an error type, the proposed correction, and several additional fields. Both annotations refer to the same span (`1 2`), covering the token *give*. The first annotation, `R:VERB:SVA`, indicates that the error is a verb replacement (`R`) motivated by a subject–verb agreement violation (`SVA`); the proposed correction is *gives*. The second annotation, `R:VERB:TENSE`, also involves a verb replacement, but the error category is tense mismatch; here the proposed correction is *gave*. The `REQUIRED` field signals that the correction is necessary for producing the gold-standard version, while `-NONE-` denotes the absence of an annotator comment. This format, originally defined for the CoNLL-2014 shared task, remains the *de facto* standard for edit-based GEC evaluation.

This intrinsic variability renders GEC fundamentally generative and evaluatively underspecified, complicating the design of robust evaluation metrics. Consequently, GEC faces similar evaluation challenges to machine translation, where a single reference may not capture the full range of acceptable outputs. This multiplicity of valid corrections necessitates metrics that are tolerant of lexical and structural variation and that can operate across multiple reference sentences.[2]

The architectural advances of GEC systems have been accompanied by increasingly sophisticated evaluation methods. Traditional metrics like MaxMatch ($\mathtt{M}^2$) (Dahlmeier & Ng, 2012) emphasized precision and recall over annotated edits.[3] Later tools, such as `errant_compare` (Bryant et al., 2017), classified edit types to provide diagnostic insights. Other metrics, like GLEU (Napoles et al., 2015), shifted focus toward fluency, while recent reference-less metrics aim to assess correction quality without relying on gold-standard outputs (Napoles et al., 2016b).

Edit-based evaluation has become the dominant approach in GEC, largely because of its interpretability: by explicitly labeling the type and location of each correction, metrics such as MaxMatch and `errant_compare` can offer fine-grained diagnostic feedback that is valuable for both system developers and pedagogical applications. These methods, however, depend on sentence-level alignment and assume minimal structural divergence between the system output and the reference. While effective in controlled settings, this reliance becomes a limitation in more flexible, prompting-based systems that frequently perform broader rewrites, modifying sentence boundaries, punctuation, or discourse structure. Under such conditions, edit-based metrics may fail to capture genuine improvements or may penalize stylistic variation that diverges from the reference. Fluency-oriented metrics attempt to address these issues, but often lack the interpretability and granularity of edit-based evaluation. As GEC systems increasingly operate at the paragraph or document level, there is a growing need for evaluation frameworks that tolerate structural variation, assess both grammaticality and fluency, and remain informative for analysis and comparison.

This chapter aims to improve the robustness, relevance, and real-world applicability of edit-based GEC evaluation methodologies. Our approach addresses the complexities of learner writing in authentic contexts, supports more reliable evaluation across diverse inputs, and better captures variation in language processing outcomes. In particular, we adopt the JP- ALGORITHM, which builds on our earlier JP- PREPROCESSING and JP- EVALB pipelines, to ensure that sentences are aligned before evaluation even in cases where preprocessing steps introduce mismatches between the source text and the annotated corrections. This alignment step is essential to maintaining evaluation integrity, particularly in end-to-end settings where tokenization or segmentation discrepancies could otherwise distort scoring.

This chapter outlines an expanded framework for evaluating grammatical error correction. We begin by reviewing existing evaluation metrics and the assumptions that underlie

---

[2] We develop the potential multi-reference evaluation methodology in Appendix B.

[3] It is useful to distinguish between $\mathtt{M}^2$, the MaxMatch evaluation metric, and M2, the file format used for grammatical error annotation.

them, with particular attention to their alignment strategies and their strengths and limitations (Sect. 5.2). We then introduce JP- ERRANT, our re-implementation of `errant`, and describe the alignment procedure used in `errant_compare`, which forms the core of our edit-based evaluation approach (Sect. 5.3). The discussion next turns to an English case study demonstrating the reliability and reproducibility of JP- ERRANT on real learner data (Sect. 5.4). A multilingual extension follows, showing how JP- ERRANT produces grammatical error annotations across typologically diverse languages without relying on language-specific resources for edit-based evaluation (Sect. 5.5).

5.2 Evaluation Principles for GEC

5.2.1 Overview of Evaluation Metric Types

Evaluation metrics for GEC assess system output by comparing it to a human-annotated reference correction. Broadly, these metrics fall into two categories depending on how they interpret the reference: *edit-based* metrics, which explicitly compare sets of minimal edits between the source and the correction, and *fluency-based* metrics, which evaluate how closely the system output resembles a fluent version of the sentence without necessarily identifying specific edits. Edit-based metrics, such as HOO (Dale & Kilgarriff, 2011), M^2 (Dahlmeier & Ng, 2012), and I-measure (Felice & Briscoe, 2015), aim to score systems based on the minimal set of grammatical edits required to transform the source sentence into the corrected reference, typically preserving its structure and phrasing. In contrast, fluency-based metrics, such as GLEU (Napoles et al., 2015) and GLEU^+ (Napoles et al., 2016a), allow more flexible rewrites to improve fluency and stylistic quality, even when these diverge from the source sentence (Sakaguchi et al., 2016). Reference-less evaluation methods (Napoles et al., 2016b), which do not rely on human-annotated corrections, have also been explored. These include grammaticality-based metrics, which use language models to estimate the well-formedness and fluency of a sentence without explicit reference annotations, in a manner similar to quality estimation in machine translation. While such methods have shown good correlation with human judgments (Napoles et al., 2016b), they are not yet as widely adopted in GEC evaluation as edit-based metrics. In this section, we provide an overview of key evaluation metrics and compare their underlying methodologies and performance characteristics.

- Helping Our Own (HOO) (Dale & Kilgarriff, 2011), which evaluates system output using an alignment and categorization scheme originally designed for error types in English learner writing.
- M^2 (Dahlmeier & Ng, 2012), which identifies the sequence of edit operations that best transforms the original sentence into the corrected reference. It computes precision, recall,

and a weighted F-score (typically $F_{0.5}$) based on matched edits and has become the standard evaluation metric in many GEC shared tasks.
- I-measure (Felice & Briscoe, 2015), which improves over $\mathtt{M}^2$ by addressing issues such as under-penalizing spurious system edits and by offering more detailed alignment diagnostics.
- GLEU and GLEU$^+$ (Napoles et al., 2015, 2016a), which adapt machine translation metrics for GEC by comparing n-gram overlap between the source, the hypothesis, and the reference(s), offering a fluency-oriented evaluation.
- Reference-less metrics (Napoles et al., 2016b), which avoid reliance on reference corrections by evaluating grammaticality and fluency directly using language models or classifiers trained to predict human acceptability, in line with approaches from quality estimation in machine translation.

In addition to these evaluation metrics, we focus on `errant_compare`, which forms the core of this chapter. We re-implement it as an alignment-based approach to support end-to-end evaluation within the edit-based GEC framework.

Figure 5.1 presents a source essay written by an English learner from MultiGEC (Masciolini et al., 2025b), alongside its system-generated correction by ChatGPT 4o, the corresponding gold-standard correction, and the associated grammatical error annotation (M2 file). The system output was produced using the following prompt:

Correct any grammatical, spelling, or punctuation errors in the following English sentence. Do not change the meaning or style unnecessarily. If the sentence is already correct, repeat it exactly.

The M2 file format is used to store grammatical error annotations. In both the $\mathtt{M}^2$ and I-measure evaluations, the gold edits are generated from the provided M2 file. The `errant` toolkit requires M2 files for both the system output and the gold standard, with edits that must be consistent between them. Therefore, while any M2 format will work, we use our own JP- ERRANT to generate the M2 files. Each block in the M2 file begins with an `S` line, which contains the source sentence. In this example, the `S` line is omitted for brevity. It is followed by one or more `A` lines, each representing an annotation, with fields separated by ||| as illustrated below.

```
A <start> <end>||| <type>||| <correction>||| <required?>||| <comment>||| <annotator_id>
                                                                  ↓ distinguishes different annotators
                                                    ↓ optional, often -NONE-
                                        ↓ usually REQUIRED
                            ↓ the corrected text (or empty for deletions)
                    ↓ it encodes the error: R: = replacement, M: = insertion (missing), U: = deletion (unnecessary)
  ↓ token indices of the error span. If start == end, it's an insertion)
```

We note that the annotation is applied to the entire essay, which is atypical, as GEC annotation is typically performed at the sentence level. In addition, all annotations are simplified compared to the original `errant` annotation (Masciolini et al., 2025a), using

SOURCE There are lots of important things in our life. However, in most cases, they depend on the priorities we have and acceptation we are awaiting from it. If it fulfils our dreams and aims or not? First of all, let us start with one of the most important things in our life and that is health. Our mind and body will be so much satisfied as we give our body at least the minimum of our time. What I am trying to say is that a certain form of physical activity per week is beneficial in many facets of our life. That is to say, If you lead an active life, your body appreciate it when you get older. On the other hand, those who prefer not to have an active life and their efforts to put their time in any kind of activity have a bad perspective when they get older. Moreover, their lifestyle is probably aimed to work and earning money. All things considered, it seems reasonable to revise our free time and to think it over, if we have what we wanted.

PREDICTION There are lots of important things in our life. However, in most cases, they depend on the priorities we have and the validation we are awaiting from them. Does it fulfill our dreams and aims or not? First of all, let us start with one of the most important things in our life, and that is health. Our mind and body will be much more satisfied if we give our body at least the minimum of our time. What I am trying to say is that a certain form of physical activity per week is beneficial in many facets of our life. That is to say, if you lead an active life, your body will appreciate it when you get older. On the other hand, those who prefer not to have an active life and do not make efforts to put their time into any kind of activity may face negative consequences when they get older. Moreover, their lifestyle is probably aimed at working and earning money. All things considered, it seems reasonable to revise our use of free time and to reflect on whether we have what we wanted.

REFERENCE There are lots of important things in our life. However, in most cases, they depend on the priorities we have and the acceptation we are awaiting from it. If it fulfils our dreams and aims or not. First of all, let us start with one of the most important things in our life and that is health. Our mind and body will be very satisfied if we give our body at least the minimum of our time. What I am trying to say is that a certain form of physical activity per week is beneficial in many facets of our life. That is to say, if you lead an active life, your body appreciates it when you get older. On the other hand, those who prefer not to have an active life and their efforts to put their time in any kind of activity have a bad perspective when they get older. Moreover, their lifestyle is probably aimed at working and earning money. All things considered, it seems reasonable to revise our free time and to think it over: do we have what we wanted?

ANNOTATION
```
A 24 24|||M:OTHER|||the|||REQUIRED|||-NONE-|||0
A 40 41|||R:OTHER|||.|||REQUIRED|||-NONE-|||0
A 69 71|||R:OTHER|||very|||REQUIRED|||-NONE-|||0
A 72 73|||R:OTHER|||if|||REQUIRED|||-NONE-|||0
A 115 116|||R:ORTH|||if|||REQUIRED|||-NONE-|||0
A 124 125|||R:MORPH|||appreciates|||REQUIRED|||-NONE-|||0
A 173 174|||R:OTHER|||at|||REQUIRED|||-NONE-|||0
A 174 175|||R:OTHER|||working|||REQUIRED|||-NONE-|||0
A 196 197|||R:OTHER|||:|||REQUIRED|||-NONE-|||0
A 197 198|||R:OTHER|||do|||REQUIRED|||-NONE-|||0
A 203 204|||R:OTHER|||?|||REQUIRED|||-NONE-|||0
```

Fig. 5.1 Example of a learner-produced sentence, its correction by ChatGPT 4o, the gold-standard correction, and associated grammatical error annotations provided by Masciolini et al. (2025a)

the generic tag `Other` instead of specific `POS` labels. Moreover, the system prediction must be tokenized, since the error annotation operates over tokenized reference sentences. This example will serve as a running case study throughout the section to illustrate how different evaluation metrics, including $\mathtt{M}^2$, `I-measure`, `errant_compare`, and GLEU assess system performance under varying alignment and annotation assumptions.

5.2.2 Edit-Based Evaluation Metrics

5.2.2.1 Helping Our Own

The Helping Our Own shared task evaluates grammatical error correction using the F_1 score computed over grammatical error annotation edits (Dale & Kilgarriff, 2011). It provides XML-style grammatical error annotation guidelines, and each participating system is required to submit a set of edits with all relevant attributes specified. Each `<edit>` element includes a unique index, an error type, and character-level `start` and `end` offsets marking the span of the edit in the original source text. It also contains an `<original>` string (the uncorrected text) and a `<correction>` list containing one or more proposed revisions. Notably, HOO uses character-based indexing rather than token-based spans, enabling fine-grained evaluation, particularly useful for punctuation, spacing, and formatting errors.

The evaluation metric aligns system edits with gold-standard edits using a strict matching criterion: both the start and end character offsets must exactly coincide. Once an edit is aligned, the system's proposed correction must match one of the reference correction strings exactly in order to be counted as a valid correction. Precision, recall, and F_1 score are then calculated over these matched edits. The framework also includes a 'bonus' mode for handling optional edits in the reference: systems are not penalized for omitting such edits and may even receive credit for choosing not to make unnecessary modifications.

Despite its structured format, HOO's evaluation scheme presents several challenges. Because alignment is based on character-level spans, even linguistically appropriate corrections may fail to receive credit if they differ in segmentation from the reference, such as when a system splits or merges edits differently. Furthermore, the specification does not clarify whether edits should be limited to single tokens or may cross token boundaries, leading to ambiguity in annotation practices. These limitations are exacerbated by the lack of publicly available technical guidelines or standardized conversion scripts, which more recent edit-based evaluation frameworks explicitly provide. As a result, reproducing HOO evaluation results can be difficult, and discrepancies across different implementations may arise due to the absence of standardized tools and technical specifications.

The use of $F_{0.5}$ weighting reflects the task's emphasis on precision over recall, favoring systems that minimize incorrect edits even if some valid corrections are missed. While $\mathtt{M}^2$ provides a clear and interpretable framework for evaluating edit overlap, it requires exact matching between predicted and reference edits, both in span and in corrected content. As a result, systems that generate correct final sentences may still be penalized when their intermediate edits differ structurally from the reference, making $\mathtt{M}^2$ sensitive to superficial mismatches in edit representation.

Figure 5.2 shows the sequence of edits derived from the system prediction by comparing the system output with the source (EDIT SEQ), the gold-standard edits from the gold annotation (GOLD EDITS), and the true positives, that is, edits correctly identified by the system. In this example, the system proposed 15 edits, of which 5 were correct, while the gold annotation contained 11 edits. This yields a precision of $\frac{5}{15} = 0.3333$, a recall of $\frac{5}{11} = 0.4545$, and an $F_{0.5}$ score of 0.3521, reflecting the evaluation emphasis on precision over recall.

Each edit is represented as a 4-tuple in the format `(start, end, source, target)`. Here, `start` and `end` denote the token offsets in the original source sentence that the edit applies to, with zero-based indexing. The `source` string refers to the tokens in the span `[start:end]` of the original sentence, and the `target` string specifies the

EDIT SEQ :	[(24, 24, '', 'the'), (24, 25, 'acceptation', 'validation'), (29, 34, 'it . If it fulfils', 'them . Does it fulfill'), (58, 58, '', ','), (69, 71, 'so much', 'much more'), (72, 73, 'as', 'if'), (115, 116, 'If', 'if'), (124, 124, '', 'will'), (146, 147, 'their', 'do not make'), (152, 153, 'in', 'into'), (157, 161, 'have a bad perspective', 'may face negative consequences'), (173, 174, 'to', 'at'), (174, 175, 'work', 'working'), (189, 189, '', 'use of'), (193, 198, 'think it over , if', 'reflect on whether')]
GOLD EDITS :	[(24, 24, '', ['the']), (40, 41, '?', ['.']), (69, 71, 'so much', ['very']), (72, 73, 'as', ['if']), (115, 116, 'If', ['if']), (124, 125, 'appreciate', ['appreciates']), (173, 174, 'to', ['at']), (174, 175, 'work', ['working']), (196, 197, ',', [':']), (197, 198, 'if', ['do']), (203, 204, '.', ['?'])]
CORRECT EDITS :	[(24, 24, '', 'the'), (72, 73, 'as', 'if'), (115, 116, 'If', 'if'), (173, 174, 'to', 'at'), (174, 175, 'work', 'working')]

Fig. 5.2 Example of edit sequences for M^2 evaluation

corrected replacement. For example, the edit `(24, 24, '', 'the')` inserts the word "the" at token position 24; `(24, 25, 'acceptation', 'validation')` replaces the word "acceptation" with "validation"; and `(29, 34, 'it . If it fulfils', 'them . Does it fulfill')` substitutes a five-token span with a rephrased expression, involving both lexical and structural changes.

We note that the M^2 scorer takes as input the plain system prediction and the gold-standard edit annotation, in contrast to the current `errant` scorer (`errant_compare`), which compares a system-generated annotation file against a reference annotation file.

When multiple gold annotations are available for a given source sentence, the M^2 scorer computes the $F_{0.5}$ score against each reference individually and selects the one that yields the highest score with respect to the system output. This best-match strategy ensures that systems are not penalized for producing corrections that align with any valid reference, thereby accounting for the inherent variability in grammatical error correction. However, it also introduces asymmetry into the evaluation, as only one reference is used per sentence during scoring, potentially underutilizing the full range of available annotations.

5.2.2.2 I-Measure

The I-measure (improvement measure) evaluates grammatical error correction at the token level by computing metrics based on alignments among the source sentence, the system hypothesis, and one or more gold-standard references. Unlike the M^2 metric, which relies on phrase-level edit extraction, I-measure employs a globally optimal three-way alignment using dynamic programming to simultaneously align tokens from the original sentence, the system output, and the reference correction. This alignment forms the basis for consistent token-level classification.

Each token in the system output is then labeled as correct, incorrect, or unchanged, allowing for the computation of both detection and correction scores using standard precision, recall, and F_β formulas. To handle ambiguous cases, particularly where a token simultaneously resembles both a false positive and a false negative, the metric introduces a special category, FPN (false positive and false negative), which is incorporated into correction evaluation but excluded from detection scoring.

To reflect the relative importance of different correction outcomes, the I-measure further introduces a weighted accuracy metric (WAcc), in which true positives and false positives are given greater weight than true negatives and false negatives. This weighting prioritizes edits that actively improve the source text over those that merely preserve it. Finally, a derived improvement score (I) quantifies the net gain (or degradation) of the system output relative to the uncorrected source, normalized by the maximum possible improvement for the given reference. This enables a more interpretable and diagnostic assessment of whether the system meaningfully improves the input text.

In I-measure, the baseline for comparison is a system that makes no corrections, that is, it simply outputs the original sentence unchanged. The improvement score (I) quantifies how much better or worse a system performs relative to this baseline, using weighted accuracy (WAcc) as the underlying metric. A positive I value indicates that the system has improved the source text beyond the uncorrected version, while a negative value suggests that the system has introduced more errors than it has corrected, effectively degrading the text quality.

The improvement score (I) quantifies how much better—or worse—a system performs relative to a baseline that makes no corrections. It is derived from the system's weighted accuracy (WAcc_{sys}) and the baseline weighted accuracy ($\text{WAcc}_{\text{base}}$), and is computed using the following formula:

$$I = \begin{cases} 0 & \text{if } \text{WAcc}_{\text{sys}} = \text{WAcc}_{\text{base}} \\ \dfrac{\text{WAcc}_{\text{sys}} - \text{WAcc}_{\text{base}}}{1 - \text{WAcc}_{\text{base}}} & \text{if } \text{WAcc}_{\text{sys}} > \text{WAcc}_{\text{base}} \\ \dfrac{\text{WAcc}_{\text{sys}}}{\text{WAcc}_{\text{base}}} - 1 & \text{if } \text{WAcc}_{\text{sys}} < \text{WAcc}_{\text{base}} \end{cases} \tag{5.1}$$

Here, weighted accuracy is computed as: $\text{WAcc} = \frac{w \cdot TP + TN}{w \cdot (TP+FP)+TN+FN-\frac{(w+1)\cdot \text{FPN}}{2}}$ where the weight w controls the relative importance assigned to successful corrections (true positives) versus the preservation of correct tokens (true negatives). Table 5.1 presents the system's weighted accuracy, the corresponding baseline value, and the resulting improvement score I derived from the alignment example in Fig. 5.3. Negative values of I indicate that the system underperforms relative to the baseline.

When multiple gold-standard annotations are available for a given sentence, I-measure evaluates the system output independently against each reference, without aggregating or synthesizing edits across annotators. For each sentence, it computes evaluation metrics—

Table 5.1 Weighted accuracy of the system and baseline, along with the resulting improvement score, for both detection and correction aspects

	$WAcc_{sys}$	$WAcc_{base}$	I
CORRECTION	80.33	94.15	−0.1467
DETECTION	81.67	94.15	−0.1326

The scores are based on the alignment shown in Fig. 5.3

SYSTEM COUNTS :	CORRECTION	`'tn': 180, 'fp': 22, 'fn': 6, 'tp': 6, 'fpn': 2`
	DETECTION	`'tn': 180, 'fp': 20, 'tp': 8, 'fn': 4`
BASELINE COUNTS :	CORRECTION	`'tn': 193, 'fn': 12`
	DETECTION	`'tn': 193, 'fn': 12`

Fig. 5.3 Example of edit sequences for I-measure evaluation

such as weighted accuracy (WAcc)—relative to each individual reference and selects the one that yields the highest score. This per-sentence best-match strategy allows I-measure to give credit for valid corrections even if they align with only one of several plausible references. By avoiding penalties for divergence from alternative but linguistically acceptable annotations, this approach supports a more comprehensive and recall-oriented evaluation framework than methods that rely on a single fixed reference.

5.2.2.3 `errant_compare`

The `errant_compare` utility (Bryant et al., 2017) is the primary evaluation script provided by the `errant` framework, designed to compare a system-generated M2 file (hypothesis) against a gold-standard M2 reference, both of which can be generated using `errant`'s automatic alignment and annotation tools. It performs span-based evaluation of grammatical error correction by aligning edits between the hypothesis and the reference, and computing standard metrics such as precision, recall, and F-score (with $F_{0.5}$ as the default, favoring precision). In addition to overall scores, it reports counts of true positives (TP), false positives (FP), and false negatives (FN), enabling fine-grained performance analysis.

A key feature of `errant` is its language-specific grammatical error classification module, which maps edits to predefined error types such as `M:PUNCT` or `R:VERB:TENSE`. This classification depends on a rule-based part-of-speech tagger, which must be configured for each language. For English, the original `errant` provides default settings that use the spaCy pipeline, but extending it to other languages requires adapting part-of-speech tag mappings and the taxonomy of error types. This language-aware classification can support more interpretable evaluation and enable targeted error analysis, allowing for the assessment of system strengths and weaknesses by specific error categories.

In `errant`, edits are classified into core types based on the relationship between source and target tokens: M (Missing) marks content that appears in the target but is absent in the source; R (Replacement) denotes substitutions where source tokens are replaced by different tokens in the target; and U (Unnecessary) identifies content in the source that does not appear in the target. These atomic operations help structure the classification of edits and support consistent labeling for error types.

The `errant_parallel` tool requires both the source sentence and its corresponding correction (either the predicted output or the gold standard) as input, and generates the corresponding M2 file containing the annotated edits. Figure 5.4 illustrates the list of annotations produced by `errant_parallel`, comparing the predicted edits with the gold-standard edits. In the figure, matching edits between the predicted and gold-standard annotations are intentionally highlighted in green to visually indicate agreement.

Table 5.2 presents the evaluation results produced by `errant_compare`, summarizing both overall and fine-grained performance metrics. The top section (CORRECTION) shows the aggregate edit-level evaluation, where edits are aligned and matched according to both their span and their assigned error type. The system achieved an overall $F_{0.5}$ score of 0.4971, reflecting its emphasis on precision, with 17 true positives (TP), 19 false positives (FP), and 10 false negatives (FN).

The middle section breaks down performance by core edit operations: M (Missing), R (Replacement), and U (Unnecessary). These categories capture the structural relationship between source and target tokens in each edit, and provide insight into which types of errors the system handles most effectively. The system performs best on replacement edits, with a precision of 0.5517 and recall of 0.6957. In contrast, it struggles with missing edits—often insertions—where both precision and recall are markedly lower. Unnecessary edits are rare in this case, resulting in sparse statistics.

The final row reports token-level detection performance, which abstracts away from specific error types and focuses on whether the system correctly identified that an error exists within a span. Detection precision and recall are higher than correction scores, yielding an $F_{0.5}$ of 0.614. This gap between detection and correction performance is typical in GEC evaluation, indicating that systems may correctly identify the presence of an error but struggle to generate an accurate correction.

Although this table does not show part-of-speech–specific results or MRU-POS intersections, the `errant_compare` framework supports such fine-grained evaluation through its detailed edit classification scheme. Additional tables can be constructed to analyze performance across specific POS-tagged error types (e.g., `R:VERB:TENSE` which denotes a replacement edit in which the morpheme expressing verbal tense in the original sentence is substituted with a different morpheme in the system output, typically to correct tense misuse or temporal disagreement), allowing for more targeted system diagnostics and error-type–level comparisons.

When multiple human references are available for the same sentence—each encoded as a separate annotation within the same M2 block and distinguished by unique annotator IDs

PREDICTION

```
A 8 10|||R:ORTH|||life . However ,|||REQUIRED|||-NONE-|||0
A 12 13|||R:ORTH|||cases ,|||REQUIRED|||-NONE-|||0
A 21 22|||R:OTHER|||the validation|||REQUIRED|||-NONE-|||0
A 26 26|||M:PRON|||them|||REQUIRED|||-NONE-|||0
A 26 27|||R:OTHER|||.|||REQUIRED|||-NONE-|||0
A 27 28|||R:OTHER|||Does|||REQUIRED|||-NONE-|||0
A 29 30|||R:MORPH|||fulfill|||REQUIRED|||-NONE-|||0
A 35 36|||R:ORTH|||not ?|||REQUIRED|||-NONE-|||0
A 38 39|||R:ORTH|||all ,|||REQUIRED|||-NONE-|||0
A 52 52|||M:PUNCT|||,|||REQUIRED|||-NONE-|||0
A 55 56|||R:ORTH|||health .|||REQUIRED|||-NONE-|||0
A 62 63|||U:ADV|||||REQUIRED|||-NONE-|||0
A 64 64|||M:ADV|||more|||REQUIRED|||-NONE-|||0
A 65 66|||R:PREP|||if|||REQUIRED|||-NONE-|||0
A 76 77|||R:ORTH|||time .|||REQUIRED|||-NONE-|||0
A 100 101|||R:ORTH|||life .|||REQUIRED|||-NONE-|||0
A 104 105|||R:VERB|||say|||REQUIRED|||-NONE-|||0
A 105 106|||M:PUNCT|||, if|||REQUIRED|||-NONE-|||0
A 110 111|||R:ORTH|||life ,|||REQUIRED|||-NONE-|||0
A 113 113|||M:VERB:TENSE|||will|||REQUIRED|||-NONE-|||0
A 118 119|||R:ORTH|||older .|||REQUIRED|||-NONE-|||0
A 122 123|||R:ORTH|||hand ,|||REQUIRED|||-NONE-|||0
A 133 134|||R:OTHER|||do not make|||REQUIRED|||-NONE-|||0
A 139 140|||R:PREP|||into|||REQUIRED|||-NONE-|||0
A 144 145|||R:VERB|||may face|||REQUIRED|||-NONE-|||0
A 145 147|||R:OTHER|||negative|||REQUIRED|||-NONE-|||0
A 147 148|||R:NOUN|||consequences|||REQUIRED|||-NONE-|||0
A 151 153|||R:ORTH|||older . Moreover ,|||REQUIRED|||-NONE-|||0
A 158 159|||R:PART|||at|||REQUIRED|||-NONE-|||0
A 159 160|||R:VERB:FORM|||working|||REQUIRED|||-NONE-|||0
A 162 163|||R:ORTH|||money .|||REQUIRED|||-NONE-|||0
A 165 166|||R:ORTH|||considered ,|||REQUIRED|||-NONE-|||0
A 172 172|||M:OTHER|||use of|||REQUIRED|||-NONE-|||0
A 176 179|||R:OTHER|||reflect on|||REQUIRED|||-NONE-|||0
A 179 180|||R:PREP|||whether|||REQUIRED|||-NONE-|||0
A 184 185|||R:ORTH|||wanted .|||REQUIRED|||-NONE-|||0
```

(36 edits)

GOLD

```
A 8 10|||R:ORTH|||life . However ,|||REQUIRED|||-NONE-|||0
A 12 13|||R:ORTH|||cases ,|||REQUIRED|||-NONE-|||0
A 21 21|||M:DET|||the|||REQUIRED|||-NONE-|||0
A 26 27|||R:ORTH|||it .|||REQUIRED|||-NONE-|||0
A 35 36|||R:OTHER|||not|||REQUIRED|||-NONE-|||0
A 36 36|||M:PUNCT|||.|||REQUIRED|||-NONE-|||0
A 38 39|||R:ORTH|||all ,|||REQUIRED|||-NONE-|||0
A 55 56|||R:ORTH|||health .|||REQUIRED|||-NONE-|||0
A 62 64|||R:ADV|||very|||REQUIRED|||-NONE-|||0
A 65 66|||R:PREP|||if|||REQUIRED|||-NONE-|||0
A 76 77|||R:ORTH|||time .|||REQUIRED|||-NONE-|||0
A 100 101|||R:ORTH|||life .|||REQUIRED|||-NONE-|||0
A 104 105|||R:VERB|||say|||REQUIRED|||-NONE-|||0
A 105 106|||M:PUNCT|||, if|||REQUIRED|||-NONE-|||0
A 110 111|||R:ORTH|||life ,|||REQUIRED|||-NONE-|||0
A 113 114|||R:VERB:SVA|||appreciates|||REQUIRED|||-NONE-|||0
A 118 119|||R:ORTH|||older .|||REQUIRED|||-NONE-|||0
A 122 123|||R:ORTH|||hand ,|||REQUIRED|||-NONE-|||0
A 151 153|||R:ORTH|||older . Moreover ,|||REQUIRED|||-NONE-|||0
A 158 159|||R:PART|||at|||REQUIRED|||-NONE-|||0
A 159 160|||R:VERB:FORM|||working|||REQUIRED|||-NONE-|||0
A 162 163|||R:ORTH|||money .|||REQUIRED|||-NONE-|||0
A 165 166|||R:ORTH|||considered ,|||REQUIRED|||-NONE-|||0
A 178 179|||R:OTHER|||over|||REQUIRED|||-NONE-|||0
A 179 180|||R:OTHER|||: do|||REQUIRED|||-NONE-|||0
A 184 185|||R:VERB|||wanted|||REQUIRED|||-NONE-|||0
A 185 185|||M:PUNCT|||?|||REQUIRED|||-NONE-|||0
```

(27 edits)

Fig. 5.4 Illustration of predicted and reference edits in the `errant` annotation format produced by JP-ERRANT, which adapts the original `errant` scheme for English

Table 5.2 Example of `errant_compare` results

	TP	FP	FN	Prec	Rec	F0.5
CORRECTION	17	19	10	0.4722	0.6296	0.4971
M	1	5	3	0.1667	0.25	0.1786
R	16	13	7	0.5517	0.6957	0.5755
U	0	1	0	0.0	1.0	0.0
DETECTION	21	15	6	0.5833	0.7778	0.614

(e.g., an integer appended to the end of each edit line)—`errant_compare` evaluates the system output against each reference independently. In the example below, the trailing `0` indicates that the edit was produced by annotator 0, and this scheme can be extended to other integer values to represent additional annotators.

```
A 21 21|||M:DET|||the|||REQUIRED|||-NONE-|||0
```

For each sentence, `errant_compare` selects the reference that yields the highest F-score relative to the system's prediction. This sentence-level best-match strategy ensures that the system receives credit for any valid correction, even if it aligns with only one of several plausible human annotations. Such a design accommodates the inherent variability and ambiguity of grammatical corrections, where multiple revisions may be equally acceptable. However, a limitation of `errant_compare`—shared with the M^2 scorer–is that it considers at most three distinct annotators when searching for the best match. By combining span-based alignment with token-level scoring and offering robust support for multi-reference evaluation (within this limit), `errant_compare` has become a widely adopted and *de facto* standard for benchmarking grammatical error correction systems.

5.2.3 Fluency-Based and Reference-less Metrics

5.2.3.1 GLEU

The Generalized Language Evaluation Understanding (GLEU) metric (Napoles et al., 2015) is a fluency-oriented evaluation measure designed specifically for GEC. It is inspired by BLEU (Papineni et al., 2002), a well-known metric in machine translation, but adapted to the monolingual rewriting nature of GEC tasks. Unlike BLEU, which evaluates system output solely based on overlap with reference sentences, GLEU incorporates the source sentence into the evaluation process. This allows it to distinguish between necessary edits (which improve fluency or correctness) and unnecessary changes (which modify already correct content).

GLEU rewards n-grams that appear in the reference but not in the source, reflecting successful corrections, while penalizing n-grams that persist from the source but should have been edited. This asymmetric treatment of source and reference better aligns with the goals of GEC, where systems are expected to make minimal, targeted modifications to improve grammaticality and fluency without introducing changes to already correct constructions. In contrast, BLEU tends to over-reward unchanged content and may assign high scores to the unedited source sentence, even when corrections are warranted.

To address certain limitations in the original GLEU formulation, GLEU$^+$ (Napoles et al., 2016a) introduces a simplified and untuned variant that remains robust across varying numbers of reference corrections. GLEU$^+$ preserves the key intuition of rewarding appropriate edits and penalizing omissions, while achieving stronger alignment with human judgments and broader applicability across evaluation settings. In this version, the traditional BLEU-style n-gram precision is replaced with a modified form that more accurately captures the quality of grammatical corrections. Specifically, the revised n-gram precision p_n is computed as:

$$p_n = \frac{\sum_{i=1}^{|D|} \max\left(0, \sum_{g_n \in h_i} \min(\rho_{i,g_n}, \eta_{i,g_n}) - \min(\sigma_{i,g_n}^{\text{diff}}, \eta_{i,g_n})\right)}{\sum_{i=1}^{|D|} \sum_{g_n \in h_i} \eta_{i,g_n}} \tag{5.2}$$

In this formulation, the evaluation is performed over a dataset D consisting of sentence triples (s_i, h_i, r_i), where s_i is the original source sentence, h_i is the system-generated hypothesis, and r_i is the reference correction. The modified n-gram precision p_n is computed across all sentence triples in the dataset.

To penalize uncorrected errors, GLEU$^+$ introduces the term $\sigma_{i,g_n}^{\text{diff}}$, which represents the portion of n-grams in the source that remain in the system output but are not supported by the reference. Formally, $\sigma_{i,g_n}^{\text{diff}}$ is set equal to σ_{i,g_n} if the n-gram g_n does not appear in the reference (i.e., it is an error that should have been corrected), and 0 otherwise. This ensures that the metric penalizes system outputs for retaining erroneous source content that has been removed or altered in the reference correction.

The numerator of p_n rewards n-grams in the hypothesis that appropriately match the reference, computed as the intersection between h_i and r_i, while penalizing n-grams that are retained from the source but do not appear in the reference. This subtraction explicitly penalizes false positives, cases where the system fails to correct erroneous n-grams from the source, thereby reducing the precision score. The use of $\max(0, \cdot)$ ensures that the numerator remains non-negative, preventing the metric from assigning negative credit. The denominator normalizes the weighted count by the total number of n-grams in the hypothesis, yielding a modified precision score that reflects both correction accuracy and fluency-preserving edits.

This formulation reflects the intuition that an effective GEC system should not only generate fluent and accurate corrections but also avoid preserving erroneous elements from the original input. The resulting GLEU$^+$ score captures this balance by rewarding necessary edits while penalizing uncorrected errors. In our evaluation, illustrated in Fig. 5.1, the system output achieved a GLEU^{+} score of 0.7532. This indicates that approximately 75% of its n-grams aligned with those in the reference correction, while successfully minimizing the retention of ungrammatical content from the source, demonstrating both strong fluency and effective grammatical correction.

5.2.3.2 Reference-less

Reference-less evaluation in GEC seeks to assess the quality of system output without relying on gold-standard reference corrections. Traditional reference-based metrics depend on explicitly annotated edits and may penalize system outputs for producing valid corrections that are not present in the reference. To address this limitation, Napoles et al. (2016b) proposed grammaticality-based metrics, which evaluate the fluency and grammatical well-formedness of system outputs independently of any reference.

Three grammaticality-based metrics are introduced: (1) ER, which leverages e-rater®'s proprietary grammatical error detection modules to count errors in a sentence; (2) LT, which uses LanguageTool, an open-source grammar checker; and (3) LFM, a ridge regression model trained on a suite of linguistic features, including misspellings, language model scores, out-of-vocabulary rates, and syntactic indicators derived from probabilistic context-free grammars and link grammars. Both ER and LT compute a normalized error rate per sentence using the formula $\text{Score} = 1 - \frac{\#\text{of errors}}{\#\text{of tokens}}$, where a higher score indicates fewer detected errors. In contrast, LFM outputs a continuous grammaticality score based on learned feature weights.

Although grammaticality-based metrics effectively capture fluency and well-formedness, they do not account for adequacy, that is, whether the meaning of the original sentence is preserved in the corrected output. To address this limitation, Napoles et al. (2016b) propose interpolated metrics that combine a grammaticality-based metric score (S_G) with a reference-based metric score (S_R), such as GLEU or $\mathtt{M}^2$. The resulting interpolated score (S_I) aims to balance grammatical correctness with semantic fidelity. It is computed as follows:

$$S_I = (1 - \lambda)S_G + \lambda S_R \tag{5.3}$$

where $\lambda \in [0, 1]$ controls the weighting between grammaticality and adequacy.

More recently, an alternative reference-less evaluation method has been proposed that leverages large language models as post-editors (Östling et al., 2025). Instead of relying on gold-standard corrections, this approach prompts a large language model to post-edit system output into a fluent and grammatical sentence. The evaluation score is then computed using a similarity metric, such as character-level 6-gram overlap, between the original system output and the large language model generated post-edited version. This strategy offers a reference-less evaluation framework that is both interpretable and effective across languages and domains, and has been shown to correlate strongly with human judgments.

This large language model based strategy offers several advantages over traditional reference-based and grammar-checker-based evaluation methods. By using the model's own correction as a dynamic reference, it avoids penalizing valid alternative corrections that may not be covered in a fixed reference set. Furthermore, since the model operates in a post-editing role, the resulting similarity score captures both grammaticality and semantic adequacy, effectively blending aspects of fluency and meaning preservation. This makes the method particularly suitable for multilingual and low-resource settings, where high-quality references or language-specific grammar checkers may be unavailable. As such, large language model based post-editing introduces a promising direction for scalable, language-agnostic evaluation of grammatical error correction systems.

5.2.4 Discussion

Evaluation metrics for GEC have evolved to meet the dual demands of linguistic precision and practical system assessment. A central divide in this landscape lies between *edit-based* and *fluency-based* metrics, reflecting a fundamental tension in evaluation priorities: whether to prioritize syntactic fidelity to annotated corrections or to reward overall linguistic acceptability and fluency. This distinction underscores differing philosophies about what constitutes a good correction—faithful reconstruction versus communicative effectiveness.

Edit-based metrics such as HOO, M^2, and I-measure prioritize alignment with gold-standard corrections, rewarding systems that perform minimal and accurate transformations of the source sentence. These approaches provide interpretable, fine-grained feedback that is especially useful in educational and diagnostic contexts. However, their dependence on exact span and token-level matching limits their flexibility, often failing to recognize valid alternate corrections that deviate structurally or lexically from the reference. I-measure offers partial mitigation of these shortcomings through token-level alignment, separation of detection and correction scores, and an improvement score that quantifies gains over a no-change baseline.

In contrast, fluency-based metrics such as GLEU and GLEU^+ shift the evaluation focus toward the output's linguistic quality. By incorporating the source sentence into n-gram comparisons, these metrics penalize unnecessary edits while rewarding successful grammatical improvements. GLEU^+ further enhances robustness by handling multiple references more consistently and improving correlation with human preferences. These metrics better align with use cases in text revision and rewriting, where fluency and readability are often more critical than edit traceability.

Reference-less evaluation represents an emerging paradigm that eliminates the dependency on annotated gold references altogether. Grammaticality-based metrics such as ER, LT, and LFM compute sentence-level fluency scores using external grammar checkers or regression models, providing a lightweight and scalable means of evaluation. While they effectively capture surface-level correctness, they do not account for semantic adequacy. To address this gap, interpolated metrics combine grammaticality scores with reference-based ones. More recently, LLM-based post-editing approaches have been proposed, wherein large language models rewrite system outputs into fluent alternatives. The similarity between original and post-edited versions is then used as an implicit measure of quality. These approaches show promising correlations with human judgments and offer a flexible, language-agnostic path forward for evaluating GEC systems.

Given this landscape, no single metric suffices for all evaluation needs. Edit-based methods offer insight into syntactic accuracy and correction behavior, while fluency- and reference-less approaches support robust and interpretable evaluation across a broader range of system outputs. A combination of metrics, tailored to the task context—such as learner feedback, automated rewriting, or benchmark development—remains the most effective strategy.

In this chapter, as mentioned earlier, we adopt `errant_compare` as the primary evaluation tool. It provides a principled, extensible framework for aligning and scoring edits in the M2 format, widely used in GEC research. Unlike surface-level metrics that operate on final outputs, `errant_compare` analyzes edits directly, enabling fine-grained error type categorization and system diagnostics. It supports hierarchical error classification and both detection- and correction-oriented scoring. Crucially, it accommodates multi-reference annotation through per-sentence best-match selection, ensuring that valid alternative corrections are appropriately credited. As a result, it has become a *de facto* standard in GEC evaluation, combining transparency, flexibility, and comparability across systems and studies.

5.3 Alignment-Based errant

5.3.1 Motivation for Alignment

In real-world GEC scenarios, sentence boundaries between the gold-standard reference and the system output frequently fail to match exactly after preprocessing. Such discrepancies can arise from a variety of sources. For instance, different tokenization rules may split or merge tokens in ways that shift sentence boundaries. Similarly, punctuation handling, such as whether quotation marks or ellipses are attached to adjacent words, can vary across preprocessing pipelines. Sentence segmentation policies, especially those implemented in off-the-shelf NLP tools, may also differ in how they treat ambiguous cases such as abbreviations, parenthetical insertions, or multi-sentence quotations. Even subtle differences in preprocessing settings can therefore lead to boundary mismatches.

If left unaddressed, these misalignments undermine the validity of evaluation. When the gold-standard and system output are segmented differently, end-to-end GEC evaluation risks comparing sentences that are only partially equivalent or, in the worst case, entirely unrelated. This can inflate error counts if overlapping corrections are mistakenly treated as separate errors, or deflate them if true errors are missed because they fall outside the mismatched comparison window. The resulting precision, recall, and F-score metrics may thus misrepresent the actual performance of the system, particularly in large-scale evaluations where manual correction of segmentation is infeasible.

To address this problem, we adopt an alignment-based approach that explicitly matches sentences in the gold-standard data to their corresponding sentences in the system output before evaluation. This alignment process operates in the preprocessing stage and takes into account both textual similarity and token sequence correspondence, ensuring that each sentence pair used for scoring is semantically and structurally comparable. By integrating alignment in this way, we retain the core evaluation measures of `errant` while guaranteeing that they are applied only to correctly matched pairs. This produces more accurate and reliable evaluations, a benefit that becomes increasingly critical in large-scale or multilingual GEC settings where discrepancies in segmentation policies are more likely to occur. Moreover, alignment offers a principled foundation for downstream error analysis, as it eliminates noise introduced by preprocessing differences and allows for a cleaner interpretation of system strengths and weaknesses.

5.3.2 Joint Preprocessing Algorithm

We build on the sentence alignment framework described in Algorithm 1, which jointly resolves sentence boundary mismatches and tokenization discrepancies between gold-standard and system outputs through a unified alignment procedure. Rather than treating boundary correction and token-level reconciliation as separate preprocessing steps, our approach integrates them into a single process, ensuring that the final evaluation operates over sentence pairs that are both structurally aligned and tokenization-consistent.

This joint method is particularly well-suited to monolingual GEC contexts, where corresponding sentences are expected to be nearly identical in content except for localized edits reflecting error corrections. In such scenarios, sentence alignment can be guided primarily by lexical and token sequence similarity, without the need to account for large-scale semantic divergence. By contrast, traditional sentence alignment techniques in machine translation must cope with much greater variability. They often rely on more complex heuristics or recursive edit operations to accommodate cases such as paraphrases, free word order, or varying sentence counts caused by translation strategies, all of which are far less common in monolingual GEC settings.

The resulting aligned and token-consistent sentence pairs form a clean input to downstream evaluation tools such as `errant`, enabling them to compute precision, recall, and F-scores without distortion from segmentation noise. In large-scale or multilingual GEC benchmarks, where preprocessing pipelines may vary widely across systems, this joint approach ensures that evaluation outcomes reflect true correction quality rather than artefacts of mismatched preprocessing.

Our alignment procedure combines deterministic pattern matching with a similarity-based decision rule to handle both exact and near matches in a principled way. The algorithm takes as input two sequences: $\mathcal{L}_i$ from the gold-standard set and $\mathcal{R}_j$ from the system output set. The first step is an exact-match check that ignores all whitespace. Two sequences are considered aligned if, after removing spaces, they are identical, as shown in Eq. (5.4).

$$\mathcal{L}_{i(\not\sqcup)} == \mathcal{R}_{j(\not\sqcup)} \tag{5.4}$$

This strict equality rule handles the majority of cases where preprocessing differences have no effect on sentence content. However, in practice, mismatches often arise from differences in tokenization policy rather than from substantive content changes. For example, the contraction *can't* may be tokenized as *ca* + *n't* in the English UD EWT corpus, but as *can* + *not* in ParTUT. In such cases, strict matching would fail despite the sequences being equivalent from a correction-evaluation standpoint.

To account for these near-matches, we introduce a modified Jaro–Winkler similarity metric that incorporates both prefix and suffix scaling. The intuition is that a high degree of similarity at the beginning and end of the strings should increase the likelihood of alignment, even if tokenization in the middle differs. We define two sequences, $\mathcal{L}_i$ and $\mathcal{R}_j$, as aligned, denoted $\mathcal{L}_{i(\not\sqcup)}$ and $\mathcal{R}_{j(\not\sqcup)}$, when their character-level similarity exceeds a predefined threshold α. In addition, the immediately following sequences, $\mathcal{L}_{i+1}$ and $\mathcal{R}_{j+1}$, must either match exactly or also meet the same similarity criterion, thereby providing local contextual confirmation as specified in Eq. (5.5).

$$(\mathcal{L}_{i(\not\sqcup)} \simeq \mathcal{R}_{j(\not\sqcup)}) \wedge \big((\mathcal{L}_{i+1(\not\sqcup)} == \mathcal{R}_{j+1(\not\sqcup)}) \vee (\mathcal{L}_{i+1(\not\sqcup)} \simeq \mathcal{R}_{j+1(\not\sqcup)})\big) \tag{5.5}$$

Formally, our modified similarity score is computed as:

$$\alpha = sim_j - \frac{(lp + l'p)(1 - sim_j)}{2} \tag{5.6}$$

Here, sim_j is the standard Jaro similarity, l and l' are the lengths of the common prefix and suffix, respectively, and p is a scaling factor (fixed at 0.1 in our experiments). Lowering α increases recall by allowing more flexible matches, but at the cost of potentially introducing false positives; conversely, raising α improves precision but risks false negatives. This trade-off can be tuned depending on the evaluation scenario–high-recall settings may be preferred in large-scale corpus evaluations, while high-precision settings may be more suitable for diagnostic error analysis.

If neither the strict nor the similarity-based matching criteria are met, the algorithm attempts a concatenation-based recovery strategy. In this stage, it progressively concatenates sequences—either from $\mathcal{L}$ or from $\mathcal{R}$—until a match is found, choosing to accumulate from the side with the shorter total length so far. This heuristic reflects the observation that sentence boundary mismatches often occur when one segmentation splits a sentence that the other treats as a single unit.

The complete procedure runs in linear time, $O(m+n)$, where m and n are the number of sentences in the gold-standard and system sets, respectively. This offers a significant efficiency advantage over traditional length-based alignment algorithms for machine translation, which operate in $O(n^3)$ time due to dynamic programming over all possible segmentations. By exploiting the near-identity of sentences in monolingual GEC contexts, our approach achieves both accuracy and scalability, making it suitable for large multilingual evaluation pipelines.

Algorithm 1 Pseudo-code for sentence alignment

function PATTERNMATCHINGSA ($\mathcal{L}$, $\mathcal{R}$):
  while $\mathcal{L}$ and $\mathcal{R}$ **do**
    if $\mathcal{L}_{i(\not\psi)} = \mathcal{R}_{j(\not\psi)}$ **then**
      $\mathcal{L}', \mathcal{R}' \leftarrow \mathcal{L}' + \mathcal{L}_i, \mathcal{R}' + \mathcal{R}_j$ where $0 < i \leq \text{LEN}(\mathcal{L}), 0 < j \leq \text{LEN}(\mathcal{R})$
    else
      while $\neg(\mathcal{L}_{i(\not\psi)} = \mathcal{R}_{j(\not\psi)})$ **do**
        if $\text{LEN}(\mathcal{L}_i) < \text{LEN}(\mathcal{R}_j)$ **then**
          $L' \leftarrow L' + \mathcal{L}_i$
          $i \leftarrow i + 1$
        else
          $R' \leftarrow R' + \mathcal{R}_j$
          $j \leftarrow j + 1$
        end if
      end while
      $\mathcal{L}', \mathcal{R}' \leftarrow \mathcal{L}' + L', \mathcal{R}' + R'$
    end if
  end while
  return $\mathcal{L}', \mathcal{R}'$

5.3.3 Sentence Re-indexing and Edit Propagation

Once sentence alignment has been completed, the resulting changes must be propagated to the associated edit annotations so that they remain consistent with the new sentence boundaries. This propagation process involves re-indexing all token positions in the edits to account for cases where sentences have been concatenated, thereby preserving the correct mapping between edits and their corresponding words.

The process consists of two steps:

1. **Re-indexing non-empty edits**: For each concatenated sentence, the token count of all preceding sentences is added as an offset to the edit indices. This ensures that edit positions reflect the updated, merged sentence structure. For example, if sentences S_i and S_j, with lengths m and n respectively, are concatenated, their edits $E_i = [e_{(a,b)}]$ and $E_j = [e_{(c,d)}]$ are transformed into $[e_{(a,b)}, e_{(c+m,d+m)}]$, where m is the offset applied to the second sentence's edits.
2. **Removing empty edits**: Following re-indexing, any edits that are empty or non-informative (e.g., `-1 -1|||noop ...`) and no longer serve an alignment purpose are removed. This produces a clean, fully aligned `m2` file ready for subsequent processing.

We re-implement `errant` with the joint preprocessing step described above, naming the resulting system JP- ERRANT. This modification integrates sentence alignment, re-indexing, and edit propagation into a single, unified preprocessing pipeline. While the original `errant` framework depends on `spaCy` for part-of-speech tagging, our version adopts `stanza` (Qi et al., 2020) owing to its strong reported performance across multiple languages.[4] Stanza's tokenization and tagging accuracy is particularly important here, as any segmentation mismatch can directly impact the edit alignment process.

The error annotation scheme itself remains unchanged from the original `errant`. However, by introducing explicit sentence alignment and index re-mapping before evaluation, JP- ERRANT ensures that all word indices in the edits correctly correspond to the updated token positions. This guarantees that evaluation metrics are computed on properly aligned data, avoiding false penalties due to misaligned boundaries.

Figure 5.5 illustrates the re-indexing process on a representative example. In the gold `m2` file, the edits consist of one empty edit and one capitalization correction (`0 1|||R:ADV`, changing *how* to *How*). However, when the same text is processed through `stanza`, segmentation mismatches result in two empty edits in the corresponding `m2` file. Applying JP- ERRANT first aligns the sentences between the gold and system outputs, then re-indexes the edits so that token positions match the merged boundaries. Finally, unnecessary empty edits (e.g., `-1 -1|||noop ...`) are removed. The result is a clean, evaluation-ready `m2` file in which edits are both positionally accurate and semantically relevant.

5.4 Case Studies

This section presents an empirical comparison of grammatical error correction evaluation on English using both `errant` and JP- ERRANT. We conduct experiments on the W&I corpus from the BEA 2019 shared task and evaluate two representative systems, GECTOR and T5.

[4] https://stanfordnlp.github.io/stanza/performance.html.

1. Preparation

```
GOLD m2     S Kate Ashby ,
            A -1 -1|||noop|||-NONE-|||REQUIRED|||-NONE-|||0
            S how are you ? I hope you are well .
            A 0 1|||R:ADV|||How|||REQUIRED|||-NONE-|||0
stanza m2   S Kate Ashby , how are you ?
            A -1 -1|||noop|||-NONE-|||REQUIRED|||-NONE-|||0
            S I hope you are well .
            A -1 -1|||noop|||-NONE-|||REQUIRED|||-NONE-|||0
```

2. Sentence alignment

```
GOLD m2     S Kate Ashby , how are you ? I hope you are well .
            A -1 -1|||noop|||-NONE-|||REQUIRED|||-NONE-|||0
            A 0 1|||R:ADV|||How|||REQUIRED|||-NONE-|||0
stanza m2   S Kate Ashby , how are you ? I hope you are well .
            A -1 -1|||noop|||-NONE-|||REQUIRED|||-NONE-|||0
            A -1 -1|||noop|||-NONE-|||REQUIRED|||-NONE-|||0
```

3. Re-indexing

```
GOLD m2     S Kate Ashby , how are you ? I hope you are well .
            A 3 4|||R:ADV|||How|||REQUIRED|||-NONE-|||0
stanza m2   S Kate Ashby , how are you ? I hope you are well .
            A -1 -1|||noop|||-NONE-|||REQUIRED|||-NONE-|||0
```

Fig. 5.5 Procedure example of JP- ERRANT: `stanza` m2 indicates that sentence boundaries are detected by `stanza` from raw text

The analysis contrasts evaluation outcomes under gold-standard sentence boundaries and system-predicted boundaries, illustrating how alignment affects precision, recall, and overall scoring. The resulting tables highlight systematic differences between the two evaluators and provide a basis for discussing the impact of alignment on reliability and interpretability in English GEC assessment.

5.4.1 English GEC Dataset

For our experiments, we utilized the development set from the Cambridge English Write & Improve (W&I) corpus, introduced as part of the *Building Educational Applications 2019 Shared Task: Grammatical Error Correction (BEA2019)* (Bryant et al., 2019). This corpus is manually annotated with Common European Framework of Reference (CEFR) proficiency levels—beginner (A), intermediate (B), and advanced (C) (Yannakoudakis et al., 2018)—providing a valuable benchmark for analyzing learner performance across different stages of language acquisition. The dataset contains texts written by L2 English learners in response to prompts, with sentence length tending to increase with proficiency: the average token counts per sentence for levels A, B, and C are 17.538, 18.304, and 19.212, respectively.

Table 5.3 Most frequent error types and their relative frequencies in the W&I dataset

Proficiency A		Proficiency B		Proficiency C	
M:PUNCT	0.0933	M:PUNCT	0.1134	M:PUNCT	0.1183
R:ORTH	0.0602	R:PREP	0.0589	R:PREP	0.0517
R:PREP	0.0506	M:DET	0.0442	M:DET	0.0345
R:VERB:TENSE	0.0455	R:VERB	0.0414	R:VERB	0.0323
R:VERB	0.0419	R:VERB:TENSE	0.0393	R:VERB:TENSE	0.0273

We conducted an error distribution analysis across these proficiency levels. At the higher levels (B and C), common error types include missing punctuation marks (`M:PUNCT`), incorrect prepositions (`R:PREP`), and missing determiners (`M:DET`), suggesting that advanced learners still struggle with fine-grained grammatical control. In contrast, beginner-level (A) data exhibits a higher frequency of orthographic errors (`R:ORTH`), such as incorrect casing or whitespace issues, reflecting early-stage writing challenges. These patterns highlight the need for evaluation approaches that account for differences in learner profiles when assessing grammatical error correction systems.

Table 5.3 summarizes the relative frequencies of the most common error types in the W&I training data, with ratios indicating their proportion in the overall grammatical error distribution (Zeng et al., 2024).

5.4.2 GEC Evaluation Results

We evaluated our approach using two off-the-shelf, state-of-the-art GEC systems: GECTOR (Omelianchuk et al., 2020) and T5 (Rothe et al., 2021). GECTOR adopts a sequence tagging framework rather than a traditional sequence-to-sequence architecture, predicting token-level edit operations directly using a Transformer encoder. This design choice results in a substantial speed advantage while maintaining competitive accuracy. In our experiments, we employed the `RoBERTa`-based GECTOR model, reported in Omelianchuk et al. (2020) as yielding the best performance among several tested Transformer backbones.[5]

In contrast, T5 (Text-To-Text Transfer Transformer) frames all NLP tasks in a unified text-to-text paradigm, enabling grammatical error correction to be treated as a conditional text generation problem. For our experiments, we used the `T5-small` variant, containing roughly 60 million parameters. This model was fine-tuned on the cleaned English LANG-8 corpus and achieved reported $F_{0.5}$ scores of 60.54 on CoNLL2014 and 65.01 on BEA2019 (Rothe et al., 2021).[6] While smaller in size than the large `T5` variants, `T5-small` still offers

[5] https://github.com/grammarly/gector.

[6] https://huggingface.co/Unbabel/gec-t5_small.

a practical trade-off between accuracy and computational efficiency, making it suitable for scenarios where speed and resource constraints are important.

The evaluation compared GEC outputs scored using the original `errant` and our JP-ERRANT implementation under two boundary conditions: gold-standard sentence boundaries and system-generated boundaries. The original `errant` is limited to gold-standard boundaries and cannot accommodate alternative segmentation, preventing a "SYS + `errant`" configuration. In contrast, JP- ERRANT can handle both gold-standard and automatically segmented input. This flexibility is essential for real-world GEC deployment, where sentence segmentation errors are common and can distort evaluation outcomes.

The results, summarized in Table 5.4, illustrate two distinct scenarios. The gold-boundary setting demonstrates that JP- ERRANT can reproduce the original `errant`'s results while integrating our joint preprocessing step. The system-boundary setting highlights JP- ERRANT's robustness to segmentation mismatches through its sentence alignment mechanism. When discrepancies between gold and system boundaries arise, JP- ERRANT performs an alignment step before re-indexing edits, ensuring that evaluation reflects genuine correction quality rather than segmentation artifacts.

We have integrated the English-specific classification module from the original `errant`, which is designed to identify and label detailed grammatical error types for English. This module extends beyond simple edit detection by categorizing errors with fine-grained labels, such as `NOUN:POSS` for possessive noun suffix errors. The classification relies on universal part-of-speech tags (Petrov et al., 2012) and dependency relation tags to determine the most specific error type possible. For example, if the first token in an edit is tagged as `PART`—typically indicating particles or other function words—and its dependency relation is `case:poss` (signaling a possessive case), the classifier assigns the label `NOUN:POSS`. By leveraging syntactic and morphological context, the module can consistently distinguish between similar-looking errors that would otherwise receive a generic label.

Although JP- ERRANT can operate without this classification module—producing generic error annotations with POS tags and enabling language-agnostic evaluation—its inclusion allows for richer, language-specific error categorization. This is particularly useful for detailed linguistic analysis, error profiling, and downstream educational applications, and it also makes it possible to develop similar classification modules for languages other than English.

While our reproduction of `errant` achieves functional equivalence, some discrepancies remain, as illustrated in Fig. 5.6. One noticeable difference is in preposition labeling: even though our system adopts the Universal POS label set, the original `errant` retains the legacy `PREP` tag instead of the Universal `ADP` tag. Another difference arises from POS tagging inconsistencies between `stanza` and `spaCy`, the latter being the tagger used by the original `errant`. For instance, in the second sentence of the example, *your* at positions 3 and 4 is tagged as a pronoun (`PRON`) by `stanza`, whereas `spaCy` classifies it as a determiner (`DET`). Such tagging differences, though infrequent, can lead to minor variations

Table 5.4 SOTA GEC results for GECTOR and T5 using the English-specific error classification module under gold and system sentence boundary conditions

GECTOR	A						B					
	TP	FP	FN	Prec	Rec	F0.5	TP	FP	FN	Prec	Rec	F0.5
GOLD + `errant`	1299	798	1680	0.6195	0.4361	0.5714	1049	621	1470	0.6281	0.4164	0.5702
GOLD + JP- ERRANT	1295	794	1678	0.6199	0.4356	0.5715	1047	623	1456	0.6269	0.4183	0.5701
SYS + JP- ERRANT	1220	842	1753	0.5917	0.4104	0.5436	1039	626	1464	0.624	0.4151	0.5670
	C						All					
	TP	FP	FN	Prec	Rec	F0.5	TP	FP	FN	Prec	Rec	F0.5
GOLD + `errant`	415	350	706	0.5425	0.3702	0.4963	2763	1769	3856	0.6097	0.4174	0.5582
GOLD + JP- ERRANT	414	350	703	0.5419	0.3706	0.496	2756	1767	3837	0.6093	0.4180	0.5582
SYS + JP- ERRANT	413	347	704	0.5434	0.3697	0.4968	2672	1815	3921	0.5955	0.4053	0.5444
T5	A						B					
	TP	FP	FN	Prec	Rec	F0.5	TP	FP	FN	Prec	Rec	F0.5
GOLD + `errant`	1271	696	1708	0.6462	0.4267	0.5859	960	593	1559	0.6182	0.3811	0.5498
GOLD + JP- ERRANT	1265	689	1708	0.6474	0.4255	0.5862	945	592	1558	0.6148	0.3775	0.5462
SYS + JP- ERRANT	1173	771	1800	0.6034	0.3946	0.5456	928	614	1575	0.6018	0.3708	0.5351
	C						All					
	TP	FP	FN	Prec	Rec	F0.5	TP	FP	FN	Prec	Rec	F0.5
GOLD + `errant`	358	350	763	0.5056	0.3194	0.4528	2589	1639	4030	0.6123	0.3911	0.5501
GOLD + JP- ERRANT	355	332	762	0.5167	0.3178	0.4592	2565	1613	4028	0.6139	0.3890	0.5503
SYS + JP- ERRANT	351	332	766	0.5139	0.3142	0.456	2452	1717	4141	0.5882	0.3719	0.5269

in the assigned error labels, underscoring the influence of upstream NLP components on GEC evaluation outcomes.

5.5 Multilingual Evaluation with JP-ERRANT

Given its demonstrated success in English, `errant` has been adapted to multiple languages, including Arabic (Belkebir and Habash, 2021), Chinese (Hinson et al., 2020; Zhang et al., 2022; Gu et al., 2025), Czech (Náplava et al., 2022), German (Boyd, 2018), Greek (Korre et al., 2021), Hindi (Sonawane et al., 2020), and Korean (Yoon et al., 2023). These adaptations have extended `errant`-style annotation to a broader range of GEC research contexts, enabling comparable evaluation protocols across diverse languages. However, extending `errant` to new languages also reveals several challenges. These include handling scripts with distinct orthographic conventions, adapting tokenization and segmentation to account for morphological richness, and mapping language-specific part-of-speech and

errant

```
S It 's difficult answer at the question " ...
A 3 3|||M:VERB:FORM|||to|||REQUIRED|||-NONE-|||0
A 4 5|||U:ADP||||||REQUIRED|||-NONE-|||0
S Thank you for your e - mail , it was wonderful to hear from you .
A 3 4|||R:DET|||your|||REQUIRED|||-NONE-|||0
A 7 9|||R:PUNCT|||. It|||REQUIRED|||-NONE-|||0
```

JP-ERRANT

```
S It 's difficult answer at the question " ...
A 3 3|||M:VERB:FORM|||to|||REQUIRED|||-NONE-|||0
A 4 5|||U:PREP||||||REQUIRED|||-NONE-|||0
S Thank you for your e - mail , it was wonderful to hear from you .
A 3 4|||R:PRON|||your|||REQUIRED|||-NONE-|||0
A 7 9|||R:PUNCT|||. It|||REQUIRED|||-NONE-|||0
```

Fig. 5.6 Differences in output between `errant` and JP- ERRANT

dependency labels to the Universal Dependencies framework without losing relevant grammatical distinctions. In languages that are highly agglutinative or morphologically complex, the default alignment and classification procedures often require substantial modification to produce accurate error categorizations. Addressing these challenges is crucial to ensuring that `errant`-based evaluation remains both reliable and linguistically meaningful in multilingual settings.

One way to address these cross-linguistic challenges is to design a consistent yet flexible error typology. An error typology provides a systematic framework for identifying, classifying, and analyzing errors in written text. We propose a two-tiered approach consisting of a language-agnostic foundation and a set of structured, language-specific extensions. The first tier follows the widely adopted MRU (Missing, Replacement, Unnecessary) framework, which ensures consistency in annotation and evaluation across different linguistic systems. The second tier provides a structured template for language-specific extensions, allowing related languages to share annotation strategies and minimize redundant reimplementation. By adopting this layered structure, we maintain standardization across languages while enabling precise refinements tailored to the grammatical properties of individual languages.

5.5.1 Language-Agnostic Error Annotation

The MRU framework classifies errors into three core operations: Missing (M), where essential elements are omitted; Replacement (R), where an incorrect element substitutes the correct one; and Unnecessary (U), where superfluous elements cause redundancy. Each error is further specified with part-of-speech tags for precise categorization.

Missing (M). An essential linguistic element is omitted from a sentence, leading to incomplete or ungrammatical structures. These errors typically involve the absence of words or phrases necessary for grammaticality or semantic clarity, such as missing determiners. In annotation, missing errors are further categorized based on part-of-speech tags or syntactic functions. For example, M:NOUN indicates a missing noun.

Replacement (R). An incorrect linguistic element is used in place of the correct one. These errors frequently involve incorrect word forms or inappropriate lexical choices (e.g., R:VERB denotes an erroneous verb substitution). To further reduce ambiguity in annotation, we implement the $\mathtt{R} : \mathtt{P}_1 \rightarrow \mathtt{P}_2$ pattern, where $\mathtt{P}_1$ is replaced by $\mathtt{P}_2$.

Unnecessary (U). A superfluous linguistic element is present in a sentence, resulting in redundancy or ungrammaticality. These errors often involve extraneous words or phrases that disrupt sentence structure or meaning. Similar to missing and replacement errors, unnecessary errors are annotated with part-of-speech information to specify the redundant element. For example, U:DET denotes an unnecessary determiner.

5.5.2 Language-Specific Error Annotation

To accommodate language-specific characteristics, we introduce a set of structured extensions to the MRU core. Our approach maintains consistency with established annotation schemes such as errant while capturing morphological and syntactic errors unique to different languages. Algorithm 2 presents our proposed classification routine for Replacement errors. Given a pair of word sequences, the source ($\mathcal{S}$) and the target ($\mathcal{T}$), the algorithm classifies the error into one of the following types: spelling errors (R:SPELL), word order errors (R:WO), or word boundary errors (R:WB). Spelling similarity is computed using two metrics: phonetic similarity and visual (shape-based) similarity. The thresholds α_1 and α_2 govern sensitivity to phonetic and visual matches, respectively.

The classification uses the following notation:

- $\mathcal{S}, \mathcal{T}$: word sequences in the source and target sentences.
- SIM(*phonetic*) and SIM(*shape*): similarity functions comparing pronunciation and visual form.
- SET($\mathcal{S}$): returns a bag-of-words representation of $\mathcal{S}$, disregarding word order.
- MERGE($\mathcal{S}$): reconstructs a character sequence from the tokenized input (i.e., merging tokens without spaces) to test for boundary alignment.

This structured yet extensible framework allows consistent error categorization across languages, while also accommodating language-specific scripts and segmentation conventions.

Algorithm 2 Pseudo-code for error classification

```
function ErrorClassification (S, T):
  if (Sim (phonetic) > α1) ∧ (Sim (shape) > α2) then
    return R:SPELL:PHONOGRAPHIC
  else if (Sim (phonetic) > α1) then
    return R:SPELL:PHONETIC
  else if (Sim (shape) > α2) then
    return R:SPELL:SHAPE
  else if (Set (S) == Set (T)) then
    return R:WO
  else if (Merge(S) == Merge(T)) then
    return R:WB
  end if
  return {R}
```

Spelling errors. We classify spelling errors by their underlying cause: sound-based phonetic similarity (R:SPELL:PHONETIC), visual resemblance in orthographic shape (R:SPELL:SHAPE), or a combination of both (R:SPELL:PHONOGRAPHIC). For sound-based phonetic errors, we introduce a transcription system to represent pronunciation, such as a pronouncing dictionary for English, *pinyin* for Chinese, or romanization for other languages. This allows us to compare words based on their phonetic similarity and identify errors caused by mispronunciation or phoneme substitution. For orthographic shape errors, we assess visual similarity by converting characters into font images and applying similarity metrics. This approach helps detect errors caused by visually similar characters, such as mistyped letters in Latin-based scripts or miswritten strokes in logographic writing systems like Chinese and Japanese. By combining these methods, we systematically classify and analyze spelling errors across different languages.

Word order errors. Word order errors are flagged when the source sequence ($\mathcal{S}$) and the target sequence ($\mathcal{T}$) contain the same set of words but differ in arrangement. In such cases, all words from the original sequence are retained, but their relative positions are altered. These errors are particularly common in languages with flexible word order, where reordering affects grammaticality or readability. Identifying and categorizing such errors enables more structured syntactic analysis and improves grammatical error correction.

Word boundary errors. Word boundary errors occur when the source sequence ($\mathcal{S}$) and the target sequence ($\mathcal{T}$) yield the same sequence after merging their respective word components.

R:SPELL:PHONETIC	*their → there*
R:WO	*You can help me → Can you help me*
R:WB	*ice cream → icecream*

Fig. 5.7 Examples of Replacement error types: phonetic spelling error (R:SPELL:PHONETIC), word order error (R:WO), and word boundary error (R:WB)

These errors typically involve incorrect spacing, where words that should remain separate are mistakenly merged, or conversely, a single word is improperly split into multiple tokens. Since the fundamental content remains unchanged but the segmentation differs, such errors impact readability, syntactic structure, and lexical integrity. Addressing these errors ensures accurate word segmentation and proper grammatical representation.

Figure 5.7 illustrates representative examples of the three major subtypes of Replacement errors classified by our algorithm.

5.5.3 Applying Universal Annotation to European Languages

Without language-specific classification modules, our grammatical error annotation system remains capable of generating generic error annotations using the core MRU framework combined with part-of-speech labels. We applied this approach to German (Boyd, 2018) and Czech (Náplava et al., 2022) to assess whether structured, interpretable annotations could still be produced in the absence of custom heuristics.

As shown in Fig. 5.8, our system improves clarity by attaching POS information to word order and punctuation errors, allowing more consistent cross-lingual comparisons. For Czech, the example highlights differences in word order (WO) annotation: our method distinguishes between auxiliary and main verbs by incorporating POS information, whereas prior work generally treated such cases as generic WO errors. By capturing the syntactic function of the words involved, our method enables more precise and interpretable annotation. A similar improvement is seen for German, where our universal framework avoids language-specific categories while maintaining clear and consistent labeling.

<table>
<tr><td>Czech</td><td>S Mám velkou rodinu , tak nemohla jsem mít naději , že něco dostanu .</td></tr>
<tr><td>PREVIOUS</td><td>A 5 7|||R:WO|||jsem nemohla|||REQUIRED|||-NONE-|||0</td></tr>
<tr><td>JP-ERRANTA</td><td>A 5 7|||R:VERB AUX -> AUX VERB|||jsem nemohla|||REQUIRED|||-NONE-|||0</td></tr>
<tr><td></td><td>('I have a big family, so I couldn't hope to get anything.')</td></tr>
<tr><td>German</td><td>S Dagegen wieder , bekommen BA Studenten die ein extra Jahr oder mehr studiert haben , leichter Jobs .</td></tr>
<tr><td>PREVIOUS</td><td>A 0 3|||R:OTHER|||Dahingegen|||REQUIRED|||-NONE-|||0
A 4 5|||U:PNOUN|||||REQUIRED|||-NONE-|||0
A 5 6|||R:NOUN|||BA-Studenten|||REQUIRED|||-NONE-|||0</td></tr>
<tr><td>JP-ERRANTA</td><td>A 0 2|||R:ADV ADV -> ADV|||Dahingegen|||REQUIRED|||-NONE-|||0
A 2 3|||U:PUNCT|||||REQUIRED|||-NONE-|||0
A 5 5|||M:PUNCT|||-|||REQUIRED|||-NONE-|||0</td></tr>
<tr><td></td><td>('On the other hand, BA students who have studied an extra year or more find jobs more easily again.')</td></tr>
</table>

Fig. 5.8 Examples of grammatical error annotation for Czech and German

Table 5.5 Comparison of operation counts (Missing, Replacement, Unnecessary) on the development sets of Czech (first 1000 sentences; Náplava et al., 2022) and German (Boyd, 2018)

		Missing	Replacement	Unnecessary	Total
Czech	PREVIOUS	693	3707	515	4915
	JP- ERRANT	695	3672	530	4897
German	PREVIOUS	1341	4406	638	6385
	JP- ERRANT	1310	4348	612	6270

Compared to previous implementations, our annotation outputs remain broadly consistent in terms of overall operation counts, with only minor variations, as shown in Table 5.5. This suggests that our universal framework based on the MRU scheme can replicate established annotation distributions. Table 5.6 lists the most frequent error annotations produced by our system alongside those from previous implementations. Our system makes the syntactic categories involved in each replacement edit explicit ($R : P^1 \rightarrow P^2$), reflecting a different annotation choice rather than a direct re-labeling of existing tags.

Future work could explore how to map between these representations to support compatibility and facilitate comparative evaluations. Another direction is to extend this annotation scheme to additional languages: because our framework leverages universal POS tags and dependency labels from `stanza`, it can be readily applied to the ten other languages in the MultiGEC dataset (Masciolini et al., 2025a) without additional customization.

5.5.4 Refining Language-Specific Annotations for Korean

Previous research on Korean grammatical error annotation has relied on extensive linguistic resources (Yoon et al., 2023). However, grammatical errors in Korean often manifest at the morpheme level, as observed in L2 writing from the National Institute of Korean Language (NIKL) corpus. In contrast, prior error annotation approaches primarily operate at the word level, which aligns with our methodology. To ensure consistency in annotation, previous work established two priority rules for assigning a single error type to each word because of the potential ambiguity in error classification, particularly when multiple error types could apply to the same token: (i) INSERTION > DELETION > others, and (ii) WS (word segmentation = WB) > WO > SPELL > SHORTEN (incorrect contraction of a word) > PUNCTUATION > OTHERS.

Building on these foundations, we implement language-specific error types based on Algorithm 2 and refine the WB (word boundary) category by introducing two subtypes: WB:M for missing spaces and WB:U for extraneous spaces. The former occurs when spaces are absent between words, causing multiple words to merge into a single unit, which can

Table 5.6 Comparison of the top 10 most frequent error annotations on the development sets of Czech (first 1000 sentences; Náplava et al., 2022) and German (Boyd, 2018)

Czech				*German*			
PREVIOUS		JP- ERRANT		PREVIOUS		JP- ERRANT	
Annotation	Count	Annotation	Count	Annotation	Count	Annotation	Count
DIACR	989	NOUN → NOUN	760	PUNCT	942	DET → DET	832
OTHER	834	VERB → VERB	465	SPELL	816	NOUN → NOUN	814
PUNCT	487	PUNCT	396	DET:FORM	693	PUNCT	800
SPELL	457	ADJ → ADJ	299	OTHER	670	ADJ → ADJ	466
VERB	271	PRON	161	ORTH	529	VERB → VERB	305
WO	227	DET → DET	101	ADP	348	DET	241
NOUN:INFL	209	ADV → ADV	100	ADJ:FORM	277	ADP → ADP	170
PRON	187	NOUN → ADJ	98	PRON	273	PRON	170
MORPH	177	PUNCT → PUNCT	95	NOUN:FORM	260	PRON → PRON	144
ORTH:CASING	124	ADP → ADP	94	DET	242	AUX → AUX	143

```
S 비행기 1음식이 안 3막였습니다 .
A 1 2|||R:NOUN -> NOUN:ADP|||음식을|||REQUIRED|||-NONE-|||0
A 3 4|||R:Orthographic|||먹었습니다|||REQUIRED|||-NONE-|||0
A 3 4|||R:VERB -> VERB|||맞았습니다|||REQUIRED|||-NONE-|||1
```

Fig. 5.9 Examples from the Korean M2 file: *I didn't eat the airplane food* (Annotator 0), and *The airplane food didn't agree with me* (Annotator 1)

obscure meaning and hinder readability. The latter arises when superfluous spaces are inserted between or within words, disrupting the natural flow of the text.

Additionally, we extend grammatical error annotation to functional morphemes, categorizing errors into (i) postposition errors (ADP), (ii) verbal ending errors (PART), and (iii) honorific suffix errors (HON). These errors are further classified into missing (M), unnecessary (U), and incorrect usage (R). Figure 5.9 illustrates corrections from two annotators: the noun phrase 음식이 *eumsig-i* ('food.NOM') is replaced with 음식을 *eumsig-eul* ('food.ACC'), annotated as `R:NOUN -> NOUN:ADP`, reflecting a case marker correction. Similarly, 막였습니다 *magyeossseubnida* is replaced with 니다 *meogeossseubnida* ('ate'), which constitutes a spelling error due to phonetic and orthographic similarity.[7]

5.5.5 Extending the Framework for Chinese

Chinese grammatical error annotation presents unique challenges due to the lack of explicit word boundaries. Previous systems (Gu et al., 2025; Zhang et al., 2022) adopt segmentation schemes based on different linguistic assumptions: for instance, LTP[8] emphasizes compound words as cohesive lexical units, whereas `stanza`, trained on the Chinese GSD treebank,[9] adopts a finer-grained, morpheme-level segmentation strategy that tends to split compound expressions into smaller units.

These design choices reflect distinct philosophies rather than flaws. However, segmentation differences can affect downstream grammatical error annotation, including both the token spans and the syntactic interpretation of the correction. For example, whether a multi-character expression like 为什么 *wèishéme* ('why') is treated as one token or multiple ((为␣什么)) influences how missing or replacement errors are classified.

To illustrate the flexibility of the framework, we adopt an LTP-style segmentation approach, which aligns more closely with native speaker intuitions about lexical units in Chi-

[7] Annotator 1 annotates a replacement with 맞았습니다 *maj-ass-seubnida* ('agreed'), altering the meaning of the sentence. This highlights a potential challenge in grammatical error annotation, namely distinguishing true errors from alternative valid expressions that modify sentence semantics.

[8] https://github.com/HIT-SCIR/ltp.

[9] https://github.com/UniversalDependencies/UD_Chinese-GSD.

Chinese GSD-based WB (Gu et al., 2025):
```
S ... 解释 为 10什么 这样 的 情况 ...
A ...
A 10 11|||R:PROPN -> PRON VERB AUX|||什么 出现 了|||REQUIRED|||-NONE-|||0
```
Correction: ... 解释 为 什么 出现 了 这样 的 情况 ...

LTP-based WB:
```
S ... 解释 7为 8什么 这样 的 情况 ...
A ...
A 7 8|||R:ADP -> ADV VERB|||为什么 出现|||REQUIRED|||-NONE-|||0
A 8 9|||R:PROPN -> AUX|||了|||REQUIRED|||-NONE-|||0
```
Correction: ... 解释 为什么 出现 了 这样 的 情况 ...
... *jiěshì wèishéme chūxiàn le zhèyàng de qíngkuàng* ...
('... explain why this kind of situation has occurred ...')

Fig. 5.10 Fragments of grammatical error anenotation examples in Chinese with different word boundaries. Fine-grained GSD-based segmentation of 为什么 *wèishéme* ('why') leads to misleading annotation 什么 出现 了 *shénme chūxiàn le* ('what has occurred'), while LTP-based segmentation 为什么 出现 *wèishéme chūxiàn* ('why occurred') provides an accurate representation

nese. While the default `stanza` pipeline uses GSD-style morpheme-level segmentation, it allows researchers to substitute alternative schemes, such as LTP's compound-word-based segmentation. This optional customization demonstrates that language-specific preprocessing decisions, such as tokenization granularity, can be adapted to better support accurate and interpretable error annotation.

We achieve this integration by re-annotating the Chinese GSD treebank with LTP-informed word boundaries and retraining `stanza` on this revised corpus. This ensures compatibility with our preferred segmentation standard while preserving the benefits of `stanza`'s POS tagging and parsing pipeline. As shown in Fig. 5.10, the resulting annotations show more consistent edit spans and error categories, especially in contexts where compound expressions are frequent.

Ultimately, this customization demonstrates the modularity of our framework: rather than enforcing a one-size-fits-all solution, we allow researchers to tailor tokenization to fit linguistic expectations, making the system more robust and adaptable across languages and segmentation conventions.

5.6 Conclusion

This work presented JP-ERRANT, an alignment-based reimplementation of `errant` that integrates a refined sentence alignment procedure, `stanza`-based preprocessing, and multilingual extensions. The proposed alignment process resolves discrepancies between gold-standard and system-generated sentence boundaries, ensuring that edits are re-indexed accurately for evaluation. In reproducing `errant` with `stanza`, we also uncovered and analyzed persistent differences, such as part-of-speech label naming conventions and tagging inconsistencies, that can influence evaluation outcomes.

Beyond the English-specific implementation, we generalized the framework for multilingual grammatical error correction, with case studies in Chinese and Korean illustrating its adaptability to languages with distinct orthographic and morphosyntactic characteristics. This generalization lays the groundwork for consistent error annotation across languages, enabling comparable evaluation in diverse linguistic settings.

By establishing a flexible yet standardized foundation for GEC evaluation, JP- ERRANT supports both current research and future developments, including language-specific error classification, integration with evaluation methods based on large language models, and broader corpus coverage. These advancements move the field closer to robust, reproducible, and cross-linguistically consistent assessment of grammatical error correction systems in real-world applications.

Acknowledgements This chapter is based on (i) "Refined Evaluation for End-to-End Grammatical Error Correction Using an Alignment-Based Approach" by Junrui Wang, Mengyang Qiu, Yang Gu, Zihao Huang, and Jungyeul Park, published in *Proceedings of the 31st International Conference on Computational Linguistics*, pages 774–785, Abu Dhabi, UAE (Wang et al., 2025), and (ii) "Multilingual Grammatical Error Annotation: Combining Language-Agnostic Framework with Language-Specific Flexibility" by Mengyang Qiu, Tran Minh Nguyen, Zihao Huang, Zelong Li, Yang Gu, Qingyu Gao, Siliang Liu, and Jungyeul Park, published in *Proceedings of the 20th Workshop on Innovative Use of NLP for Building Educational Applications (BEA 2025)*, pages 202–212, Vienna, Austria (Qiu et al., 2025). The current version of JP- ERRANT builds upon the framework introduced by Qiu et al. (2025), which extends the `errant` toolkit with multilingual annotation capabilities covering a range of languages and error types. This implementation incorporates our alignment and evaluation enhancements, and the complete source code is publicly available at https://github.com/open-writing-evaluation/jp_errant_bea to facilitate reproducibility and further research. By integrating alignment into edit comparison, JP- ERRANT extends the JP-framework to end-to-end grammatical error correction evaluation.

Conclusion: Beyond Alignment-Based Evaluation 6

This final chapter reflects on the broader implications of the JP- FRAMEWORK and outlines possible directions for future evaluation research. While the preceding chapters have shown how alignment-based preprocessing restores comparability across segmentation-sensitive tasks, evaluation itself continues to evolve as modern NLP moves from discrete to representational systems. Contemporary models no longer operate on static linguistic units but on fluid, learned representations that encode syntax, semantics, and discourse within high-dimensional spaces. Evaluating such systems requires new principles that connect symbolic accuracy with representational correspondence.

The discussion that follows extends beyond alignment as an algorithmic procedure. It considers alignment as a conceptual bridge, a means of defining equivalence between structures, meanings, and model-internal representations. By reinterpreting evaluation through this lens, we can begin to envision frameworks that assess not only the outcomes of language processing but also the consistency and interpretability of the representations that underlie them.

Revisiting the motivation. These themes set the stage for revisiting the motivations that guided the development of the JP- FRAMEWORK. Throughout this book, evaluation has been treated not as a mere numerical comparison but as a process of establishing structured correspondence between linguistic representations. Traditional metrics, from token-level accuracy to F-measure and BLEU, assume that the compared sequences share identical segmentation and structure. This assumption once held for modular pipelines where each component, such as the tokenizer, parser, or corrector, operated on standardized units.

The motivation behind the JP- APPROACH arises precisely where this assumption fails. In end-to-end architectures, linguistic structure is no longer predefined but emerges dynamically from model training. Outputs that differ in segmentation or surface realization may nonetheless express equivalent syntactic or semantic content. Conventional evalua-

J. Park, *Evaluation by Alignment*, Synthesis Lectures on Computer Science,
https://doi.org/10.1007/978-3-032-16563-3_6

tion frameworks, however, penalize these differences as errors, conflating representation mismatch with linguistic divergence.

The JP- APPROACH addresses this foundational issue by redefining evaluation as an alignment problem. Rather than assuming a one-to-one correspondence between reference and system units, it seeks to establish correspondence dynamically through an alignment predicate that abstracts away from segmentation inconsistencies. This principle applies uniformly across linguistic levels, including preprocessing, syntactic parsing, and grammatical error correction.

From alignment to representation. Alignment, however, is not the endpoint of evaluation theory but a foundational step toward a deeper understanding of linguistic correspondence. It formalizes the principle that comparison must be preceded by structural reconciliation. The JP- FRAMEWORK operationalizes this principle at the surface level, aligning sentences and words so that evaluation reflects linguistic equivalence rather than segmentation consistency. Yet the same idea extends far beyond surface alignment.

Modern neural architectures produce outputs that are not limited to discrete linguistic symbols but encoded as distributed vectors in high-dimensional space. Traditional evaluation metrics are still designed for discrete comparisons: they measure overlap in words, n-grams, or labeled spans. This mismatch between representational depth and evaluative granularity reveals the limits of current approaches.

Extending alignment to representation means redefining correspondence in terms of relational similarity rather than string identity. Instead of aligning explicit tokens, future evaluation algorithms may align regions of latent space, clusters of contextual embeddings, syntactic subspaces, or semantic role configurations. Such an approach would reveal whether two systems, trained on different data or optimized for different tasks, converge on comparable internal representations of linguistic structure.

Limitations of current metrics. Conventional evaluation metrics, though foundational to the progress of NLP, are constrained by the assumptions under which they were designed. Metrics such as BLEU, ROUGE, GLEU and chrF quantify similarity through surface-level n-gram overlap, rewarding lexical and phrasal matches between system and reference. However, their simplicity limits interpretability: they measure formal resemblance rather than linguistic equivalence. The JP- ALGORITHM addresses one fundamental aspect of this broader problem, namely boundary inconsistency. By realigning system outputs and references prior to scoring, it restores fairness and interpretability for segmentation-sensitive tasks. Yet it remains bound to the discrete space of symbolic units, while modern neural models rely on continuous, context-dependent representations. This is precisely the boundary at which surface alignment becomes insufficient and representation-level correspondence becomes necessary.

Toward model-aware evaluation. A promising direction for future work is the development of hybrid evaluation metrics that combine symbolic alignment with representation-level similarity. While the JP- FRAMEWORK resolves mismatches at the level of linguistic form, emerging evaluation methodologies must also account for how models internally encode and transform these forms. Contextualized embeddings derived from transformer models already capture fine-grained syntactic and semantic relations, offering a basis for alignment between model-internal states rather than between output tokens.

Another important direction is the extension of the JP- FRAMEWORK to multilingual and cross-lingual evaluation. In multilingual settings, alignment becomes both a theoretical and practical bridge between languages with divergent structures, scripts, and segmentation conventions. This perspective situates alignment at the intersection of linguistic theory and neural representation, transforming evaluation from a tool of measurement into a framework for interpreting how models internalize linguistic structure.

Closing reflections. The JP- FRAMEWORK advances the central idea of evaluation by alignment, treating comparison as a correspondence problem rather than as a surface matching task. By mapping system outputs to reference structures across diverse linguistic conditions, it provides a common foundation for preprocessing evaluation (JP- PREPROCESSING), syntactic analysis (JP- EVALB), and grammatical error correction (JP- ERRANT), integrating previously separate paradigms into a single, coherent theory. This perspective clarifies how robust end-to-end NLP assessment can be achieved when evaluation is grounded in structural reconciliation rather than in fixed assumptions about segmentation or form.

A further implication of this view is its relevance for fully integrated, end-to-end systems, where tokenization, analysis, and correction emerge jointly during model training. In such settings, outputs may differ from reference forms in segmentation or realization while still expressing equivalent content. By anchoring evaluation in alignment, the JP- FRAMEWORK offers a principled basis for assessing these systems without penalizing superficial variation.

Beyond its immediate applications, the framework also raises a broader question about what it means for a system to represent, understand, or generate language. As models become increasingly representational, producing outputs shaped by high-dimensional contextual and semantic structure, evaluation must evolve accordingly. The next phase of research will require a transition from alignment between surface forms to alignment between representations, linking the symbolic rigor of linguistic theory with the generalization power of modern neural models. Only through such integrative approaches can evaluation remain both interpretable to humans and faithful to the representational nature of contemporary language systems.

Comparison with the Gale–Church Algorithm

A

This appendix compares the Gale–Church algorithm (Gale & Church, 1993) with the JP-algorithm in the task of sentence alignment. The goal is to illustrate how the proposed alignment method performs in a monolingual setting, where structural and segmentation differences are common even when the sentences share the same lexical content. By examining both algorithms under identical conditions, we highlight the efficiency and robustness of the JP-algorithm and show how it improves upon the assumptions and behavior of the traditional Gale–Church approach.

A.1 Extended Gale–Church Algorithm

The original Gale–Church algorithm runs in $O(nm)$ time with constant branching (1:1, 1:2, 2:1, 2:2). Our extension generalizes this to m:n groupings. With fixed caps on m and n, the branching factor remains constant and both time and space complexities stay $O(nm)$. If the caps grow with sequence length, the branching factor B increases with the number of admissible local patterns, and the worst-case time becomes $O(nm \cdot B)$.

At each step, the dynamic programming state $D(i, j)$ represents the minimal cumulative alignment cost up to the i-th and j-th sentences in the two documents. The recurrence relation is defined as the minimum over all admissible alignment patterns, excluding the 1:0 and 0:1 cases:

J. Park, *Evaluation by Alignment*, Synthesis Lectures on Computer Science,
https://doi.org/10.1007/978-3-032-16563-3

$$D(i, j) = \min \begin{cases} D(i-1, j-1) + \textsc{cost}(1{:}1, L_i, R_j) \\ D(i-1, j-2) + \textsc{cost}(1{:}2, L_i, R_{j-1}, R_j) \\ D(i-2, j-1) + \textsc{cost}(2{:}1, L_{i-1}, L_i, R_j) \\ D(i-2, j-2) + \textsc{cost}(2{:}2, L_{i-1}, L_i, R_{j-1}, R_j) \\ \vdots \\ D(i-m, j-n) + \textsc{cost}(m{:}n, L_{i-m+1..i}, R_{j-n+1..j}) \\ \vdots \end{cases}$$

Here, $\textsc{cost}(m{:}n, L_{i-m+1..i}, R_{j-n+1..j})$ denotes the local alignment cost for mapping m consecutive sentences from the left sequence to n consecutive sentences from the right sequence. The cost may incorporate sentence length ratios, character similarity, or any auxiliary metric consistent with the MATCHEDCASES predicate in Sect. A.2. This extension therefore generalizes the original Gale–Church formulation while maintaining the same asymptotic behavior under bounded m, n values.

A.2 Implementation Details

The implementation follows the same COST function and parameterization as the original Gale–Church algorithm, but extends the search to general $m{:}n$ patterns. Because this expansion increases the number of admissible local alignments, we introduce the following pruning constraint:

$$L_{i \not\sqcup} = R_{j \not\sqcup} \tag{A.1}$$

The operator $\not\sqcup$ removes all whitespace characters from both strings before comparison. This constraint restricts the search to candidate pairs whose space-removed forms match exactly or fall within a predefined similarity threshold, substantially reducing the number of valid transitions in the dynamic program.

We also recalibrate the prior probability of a sentence match, $P(\text{match})$, which in the original Gale–Church formulation is estimated empirically. In our implementation, this probability is re-estimated using sentence statistics from the `UD_English-EWT` corpus, processed with `stanza` for sentence boundary detection. This adjustment increases the estimated probability of a 1:1 match from 0.89 in the original model to 0.95.

Finally, we apply simple Laplace smoothing to handle unseen match patterns. The maximum match count is capped at 11, which allows cases such as 9:11 alignments while preventing probability underflow in rare long-sequence matches.

Table A.1 Sentence alignment accuracy on the W&I development dataset using the extended Gale–Church (EGC) and JP algorithms

	# of aligned sentences			Similarity scores		
	A	B	C	A	B	C
GOLD	957	1209	1015	1.000	1.000	1.000
EGC	933	1193	999	0.993	0.997	0.996
JP	948	1201	1008	1.000	1.000	1.000

A.3 Alignment Result Comparison

We evaluate the proposed sentence alignment approach within the joint preprocessing framework by computing the similarity between source and target texts after alignment. The similarity measure defined in Eq. A.2 quantifies how closely the aligned sentence pairs correspond, serving as an indicator of alignment accuracy for downstream processing tasks.

$$\text{Similarity} = \frac{\sum \text{similarity of each aligned pair}}{\#\,\text{of aligned sentence pairs}} \tag{A.2}$$

To calculate the similarity, each pair of aligned sentences is concatenated, all whitespace characters are removed, and the normalized edit similarity ratio is computed. Table A.1 presents the results for the Cambridge English Write & Improve (W&I) development dataset. Across all CEFR proficiency levels, both algorithms yield near-perfect similarity scores, with the JP algorithm achieving exact correspondence between gold and system sentences.

The evaluation uses the development set of the Cambridge English Write & Improve (W&I) corpus, introduced in the *Building Educational Applications 2019 Shared Task: Grammatical Error Correction (BEA2019)* (Bryant et al., 2019). The dataset is manually annotated with Common European Framework of Reference (CEFR) proficiency levels—beginner (A), intermediate (B), and advanced (C) (Yannakoudakis et al., 2018). Texts written by L2 English learners show an increase in sentence length with proficiency: the average token counts per sentence for levels A, B, and C are 17.538, 18.304, and 19.212, respectively.

We further analyze the composition of each alignment pair to observe how the algorithm handles sentence merging and splitting. Table A.2 summarizes the distribution of local alignment types, showing that most alignments are of the 1:1 type, while smaller proportions of 1:2, 2:1, and longer alignments capture sentence restructuring phenomena across proficiency levels.

Table A.2 Distribution of local alignment types across CEFR proficiency levels

	A		B		C		All levels	
	Count	Ratio (%)	Count	Ratio (%)	Count	Ratio (%)	Count	Ratio (%)
(1, 1)	853	89.13	1109	91.73	938	92.41	2900	91.86
(1, 2)	43	4.49	38	3.16	30	2.98	111	3.52
(2, 1)	27	2.85	25	2.08	24	2.38	76	2.41
Beyond	25	2.64	29	2.33	16	1.59	70	2.22

A.4 Conclusion

The comparison between the extended Gale–Church algorithm and the JP algorithm shows that both methods perform well, but the JP algorithm provides a closer match to the gold reference. The extended Gale–Church model benefits from its ability to handle general m:n alignments and from improved match priors, but it is still affected by differences in sentence structure and segmentation. The JP algorithm, by contrast, resolves these inconsistencies before scoring, which allows it to reach exact similarity across all levels. Overall, the results suggest that an alignment-aware preprocessing step offers a more stable and reliable foundation for sentence alignment in monolingual evaluation, especially when working with data that may contain inconsistent boundaries due to differences in preprocessing.

A Formal Framework for Multi-reference Evaluation

B

B.1 Introduction

Evaluation of natural language systems is inherently difficult when an input does not admit a single unique output. For many tasks, including translation, summarization, correction, and paraphrasing, there exist multiple valid realizations that differ in lexical choice, phrasing, or stylistic preference while preserving an intended meaning or function. This multiplicity raises a fundamental question: how should evaluation be defined when system outputs align with some, but not all, legitimate human variants?

Most widely used evaluation practices adopt a single-reference perspective. A system output is compared against one designated reference using a base similarity measure, such as edit overlap, span matching, or n-gram precision. This setup implicitly privileges the chosen reference as a canonical target. Outputs that are fluent and semantically appropriate, but happen to align more closely with alternative human variants, may nevertheless receive low scores. The resulting evaluation is sensitive to arbitrary choices in reference selection and may underestimate the quality of legitimate but non-canonical outputs.

Multi-reference evaluation seeks to address this limitation by comparing a system output against a set of human-produced variants rather than a single reference. A single reference captures only one realization among many possible acceptable forms. Aggregating over multiple references can reduce spurious penalization, increase robustness to stylistic and structural diversity, and improve comparability across languages that differ in morphology, word order, or segmentation. However, existing multi-reference practices often rely on heuristic schemes such as naïve averaging or ad hoc pooling of statistics. These schemes rarely make explicit what formal properties multi-reference evaluation should satisfy, or how different aggregation choices affect fairness, stability, or linguistic coverage.

This chapter develops a general mathematical framework for multi-reference evaluation that is independent of any specific task or metric. We view evaluation as an aggregation

J. Park, *Evaluation by Alignment*, Synthesis Lectures on Computer Science,
https://doi.org/10.1007/978-3-032-16563-3

problem over sets of valid linguistic variants. Given a base similarity function that scores a system output relative to a single reference, multi-reference evaluation is defined as an aggregation operator that combines the resulting set of scores (or representations) into a single value. Within this formulation, we introduce four abstract aggregation strategies—SELECT-BEST, SIMPLE- AVERAGE, WEIGHTED- AVERAGE, and MERGED- COUNTS—and analyze their mathematical properties and interpretive consequences. Concrete evaluation metrics based on edits, n-grams, or embeddings then appear as specific instantiations of the underlying framework rather than as isolated heuristics.

The goals of this chapter are threefold. First, we formalize multi-reference evaluation as an aggregation function over sets of valid variants, making explicit the structural assumptions that underlie common practices. Second, we identify and study desiderata such as boundedness, monotonicity, non-penalization, and permutation invariance, and use them to characterize families of admissible aggregation operators. Third, we show how different aggregation strategies occupy distinct positions along axes such as precision versus recall and selectivity versus inclusivity, providing a principled basis for choosing and interpreting multi-reference evaluation schemes.

By abstracting away from any particular task or metric, the proposed framework offers a unified perspective on how multiple human references can be integrated into a single, interpretable score. It thus provides a theoretical foundation for multi-reference evaluation that can be instantiated in diverse settings, from string-based similarity measures to representation-based comparisons in modern neural models.

B.2 Multi-reference Evaluation

This section introduces a general framework for evaluating system outputs in settings where multiple valid realizations may exist for the same input. Rather than assuming a single canonical reference, multi-reference evaluation integrates information from a set of human-produced variants. The goal is to provide an assessment that is robust to lexical, structural, and stylistic diversity, and that better reflects the multiplicity inherent in natural language.

B.2.1 From Single-reference to Multi-reference Evaluation

Traditional evaluation practices typically compare a system output against a single reference. This comparison may be based on edit distance, structural alignment, n-gram overlap, representation similarity, or any other base metric. While such approaches are easy to implement and interpret, they implicitly treat the chosen reference as the unique gold standard. Outputs that match alternative but equally valid human realizations may be underestimated, and evaluation becomes sensitive to arbitrary choices in reference selection.

Single-reference evaluation also assumes that the compared sequences share similar segmentation, structure, and granularity. Small discrepancies in tokenization, word ordering, or phrasing can lead to large variations in score even when the meanings or functional roles of the outputs are aligned. In multilingual, generative, or open-ended tasks, where acceptable outputs may vary widely, these sensitivities become particularly limiting.

Multi-reference evaluation addresses these issues by replacing the notion of a single authoritative reference with a set of valid human variants. Each variant provides a different perspective on what constitutes an acceptable output. Aggregating over multiple references reduces spurious penalization, increases robustness to linguistic diversity, and better approximates the range of acceptable human judgments.

However, the shift to multi-reference evaluation introduces a new methodological question: *How should a set of reference comparisons be aggregated into a single evaluation score?* Simple averaging, maximum selection, or naïve pooling of statistics are commonly used in practice, but these approaches lack explicit theoretical grounding. They do not specify what structural properties a valid aggregation function should satisfy, nor how different aggregation choices influence interpretability, fairness, or stability.

B.2.2 Multi-reference Evaluation as Aggregation

We formalize multi-reference evaluation as an aggregation problem. Let a base similarity function assign a score to a system output when compared to a single reference. Given multiple references, the evaluation problem becomes:

$$\text{Given } \{s_1, s_2, \ldots, s_n\}, \text{ how should these scores be combined into a single value?}$$

The aggregation operator determines how individual reference comparisons contribute to the final score. Different aggregation strategies correspond to different evaluation philosophies:

- a *selective* view, in which matching any one valid reference is sufficient;
- an *inclusive* view, in which all references contribute equally;
- a *probabilistic* view, in which references are weighted according to their representativeness;
- a *coverage-based* view, in which all attested linguistic material is treated as jointly defining the acceptable output space.

To capture these perspectives, we introduce four abstract aggregation strategies: SELECT-BEST, SIMPLE- AVERAGE, WEIGHTED- AVERAGE, and MERGED- COUNTS. Each operates over the set of single-reference scores and embodies a distinct interpretation of linguistic validity, precisionâŁ"recall balance, and representational diversity.

This abstraction is independent of any particular evaluation metric. Whether the base score is derived from overlap counts, structural similarity, embedding distances, or learned discriminators, the aggregation framework applies uniformly. In this way, multi-reference evaluation emerges not as a task-specific extension of existing metrics, but as a general theory of how multiple human variants can jointly guide the assessment of system outputs.

B.3 Aggregation Strategies for Multi-reference Evaluation

This section introduces the aggregation strategies used to extend any base evaluation metric to multi-reference settings. When multiple valid human outputs exist for the same input, the central challenge is determining how these distinct variants should be integrated into a single, interpretable score. We describe the general evaluation pipeline and formalize four aggregation operators that combine individual reference comparisons into a unified multi-reference evaluation.

B.3.1 Evaluation Pipeline

The multi-reference evaluation pipeline proceeds in three steps:

1. Compute the base metric $f(H, R_i)$ between the system output H and each reference R_i.
2. Combine the resulting set of scores

$$\{f(H, R_i)\}_{i=1}^{n}$$

   using one of the aggregation operators defined below.
3. Average sentence-level scores to obtain a corpus-level result.

This procedure preserves the interpretability of the underlying metric while enabling systematic evaluation across multiple human variants. The choice of aggregation operator determines how linguistic diversity, stylistic variation, and reference imbalance affect the final score.

B.3.2 Multi-reference Aggregation Strategies

We define four aggregation strategies, each reflecting a distinct evaluation philosophy. Formally, all strategies instantiate a mapping

$$\Phi : \{f(H, R_i)\}_{i=1}^{n} \rightarrow [0, 1]$$

subject to axioms such as boundedness, monotonicity, and non-penalization.

B.3.2.1 Select-best

The SELECT- BEST operator evaluates the hypothesis against each reference independently and returns the highest score:

$$\Phi_{\text{SELECT- BEST}}(H, \{R_i\}) = \max_i f(H, R_i).$$

This strategy provides an oracle-style upper bound. It is precision-oriented: the output is considered valid if it matches any one reference sufficiently well. It satisfies boundedness and monotonicity with respect to the reference set, but not fairness, since all non-maximal references are ignored.

B.3.2.2 Simple Average

The SIMPLE- AVERAGE operator assigns equal weight to all references:

$$\Phi_{\text{SIMPLE- AVG}}(H, \{R_i\}) = \frac{1}{n}\sum_{i=1}^{n} f(H, R_i).$$

This strategy emphasizes representational balance and treats all references as equally plausible. It satisfies boundedness, symmetry, and fairness, but may violate monotonicity: adding a low-scoring reference can reduce the overall score. It corresponds to a collective interpretation of acceptability.

B.3.2.3 Weighted Average

The WEIGHTED- AVERAGE operator defines a softmax-weighted combination of individual reference scores:

$$w_i = \frac{\exp(\tau \cdot f(H, R_i))}{\sum_{j=1}^{n} \exp(\tau \cdot f(H, R_j))} \qquad \tau > 0,$$

$$\Phi_{\text{WEIGHTED- AVG}}(H, \{R_i\}) = \sum_{i=1}^{n} w_i\, f(H, R_i).$$

As $\tau \to 0$, the operator converges to SIMPLE- AVERAGE; as $\tau \to \infty$, it converges to SELECT- BEST. This strategy models graded acceptability, giving greater weight to prototypical or majority-like references while still recognizing less frequent variants. It satisfies boundedness and non-penalization.

B.3.2.4 Merged Representations

The MERGED operator aggregates reference information at the representation level rather than at the score level. Let $\mathcal{R}_\cup$ denote a merged representation constructed from all references (e.g., a union of n-grams, structural fragments, or semantic units). The final score is computed using this unified representation:

$$\Phi_{\text{MERGED}}(H, \{R_i\}) = f(H, \mathcal{R}_\cup).$$

This strategy rewards overlap with any attested linguistic material and is inherently recall-oriented. It ensures monotonicity and non-penalization, since $\mathcal{R}_\cup$ expands as more references are added. Fairness may be violated, since longer or denser references contribute more material to $\mathcal{R}_\cup$.

B.3.3 Comparative Interpretation

Each strategy corresponds to a distinct view of linguistic validity:

- SELECT- BEST represents an existential perspective: correctness is satisfied by matching one valid variant.
- SIMPLE- AVERAGE adopts an egalitarian perspective: all variants contribute equally.
- WEIGHTED- AVERAGE models human-like graded preference structures.
- MERGED adopts a union-based perspective prioritizing coverage and inclusivity.

These operators define a continuum between precision-oriented and recall-oriented evaluation, clarifying how different assumptions about linguistic diversity shape the resulting scores.

B.3.4 Theoretical Foundations

Let $f(H, R_i)$ denote a single-reference score and $\mathcal{R} = \{R_1, \ldots, R_k\}$ the set of references. A multi-reference evaluator is an aggregation operator

$$F(H, \mathcal{R}) : \mathcal{H} \times 2^{\mathcal{R}} \rightarrow [0, 1]$$

that satisfies core axioms:

1. **Boundedness:** $0 \leq F(H, \mathcal{R}) \leq 1$.
2. **Monotonicity:** If each $f(H, R_i) \leq f'(H, R_i)$, then $F(H, \mathcal{R}) \leq F'(H, \mathcal{R})$.
3. **Non-penalization:** $F(H, \mathcal{R} \cup \{R'\}) \geq F(H, \mathcal{R})$.
4. **Permutation invariance:** The order of references does not affect F.

Table B.1 Analytical properties of multi-reference aggregation strategies

	SELECT BEST	SIMPLE AVG	WEIGHTED AVG	MERGED REP
Recall dominance	–	–	–	✓
Oracle upper bound	✓	–	–	–
Permutation invariance	–	✓	–	✓
Stability under representation fusion	–	–	–	✓

Within this space, the MERGED operator uniquely preserves recall dominance and convexity of representational coverage, linking multi-reference evaluation to the general theory of aggregation over bounded lattices (Grabisch et al., 2009).

B.3.5 Analytical Properties

The four aggregation operators exhibit distinct formal behaviors that determine how they respond to reference diversity and representational overlap. Table B.1 summarizes their analytical properties.

The SELECT- BEST operator represents the most selective interpretation of correctness, while the MERGED operator is the most inclusive. The SIMPLE- AVERAGE and WEIGHTED-AVERAGE operators provide interpretable intermediate points, capturing different balances between stylistic diversity, representational coverage, and precision.

Overall, these aggregation strategies characterize a principled, metric-agnostic framework for multi-reference evaluation across diverse tasks and languages.

B.4 Mathematical Formulation and Properties of Aggregation Functions

This section provides the formal definitions and analytical properties of the aggregation operators used in multi-reference evaluation.

B.4.1 Formal Definition

Let H denote the system output and $\mathcal{R} = \{R_i\}_{i=1}^{n}$ the set of reference variants associated with the same input. For each reference R_i, define a single-reference score

$$f_i = f(H, R_i) \in [0, 1].$$

A general multi-reference metric $\mathcal{F}$ can then be expressed as a mapping

$$\mathcal{F}(f_1, \ldots, f_n) = \Phi(f_1, \ldots, f_n),$$

where Φ denotes an aggregation operator satisfying four desiderata: *boundedness*, *monotonicity*, *symmetry*, and *consistency* with the single-reference case.

The four aggregation strategies instantiate $\mathcal{F}$ under distinct functional forms:

$$\mathcal{F}_{\text{SELECT- BEST}} = \max_i f_i,$$

$$\mathcal{F}_{\text{SIMPLE- AVG}} = \tfrac{1}{n} \sum_i f_i,$$

$$\mathcal{F}_{\text{WEIGHTED- AVG}} = \sum_i w_i f_i,$$

$$\mathcal{F}_{\text{MERGED}} = f(H, \mathcal{R}_{\cup}),$$

where $\mathcal{R}_{\cup}$ denotes a merged representation built from all references (for example, a union of representational units such as n-grams, structural fragments, or semantic roles). Each formulation inherits *boundedness* and *monotonicity* from the underlying single-reference metric f, while differing in *symmetry* and sensitivity to reference variation. Formally, $\mathcal{F}_{\text{SELECT- BEST}}$ provides a precision-oriented upper bound, $\mathcal{F}_{\text{MERGED}}$ a recall-oriented bound focused on coverage, and the averaging-based methods interpolate between these extremes.

B.4.2 Analytical Properties

We next formalize the analytical behavior of the aggregation operators. Each property specifies a structural constraint or monotonicity condition that governs how multi-reference scores evolve as the number and distribution of references vary.

Property B.1 (Oracle upper bound) Let $f_i \in [0, 1]$. For any $\{f_i\}_{i=1}^n$,

$$\mathcal{F}_{\text{SELECT- BEST}}(f_1, \ldots, f_n) = \max_i f_i,$$

$$\mathcal{F}_{\text{SIMPLE- AVG}}(f_1, \ldots, f_n) \leq \max_i f_i.$$

If $w_i \geq 0$ and $\sum_i w_i = 1$, then

$$\mathcal{F}_{\text{WEIGHTED- AVG}} = \sum_i w_i f_i \leq \max_i f_i.$$

Proof sketch The maximum is an upper bound by definition. Both simple and weighted averages are convex combinations, so they cannot exceed the maximum element. □

Interpretation SELECT- BEST represents an oracle upper bound, giving the highest possible score among references. Averaging methods are bounded above by the best reference and may underestimate system performance when reference diversity is high. □

Property B.2 (Monotonicity with respect to reference number) Let $\mathcal{R}_n = \{R_i\}_{i=1}^{n}$ and $\mathcal{R}_{n+1} = \mathcal{R}_n \cup \{R_{n+1}\}$. Then

$$\mathcal{F}_{\text{SELECT- BEST}}(\mathcal{R}_{n+1}) \geq \mathcal{F}_{\text{SELECT- BEST}}(\mathcal{R}_n),$$
$$\mathcal{F}_{\text{MERGED}}(\mathcal{R}_{n+1}) \geq \mathcal{F}_{\text{MERGED}}(\mathcal{R}_n).$$

□

Proof sketch Adding a reference cannot reduce the maximum in SELECT- BEST. For MERGED, the unified representation $\mathcal{R}_{\cup}^{(n+1)} = \mathcal{R}_{\cup}^{(n)} \cup U(R_{n+1})$ (for some representation function U) enlarges or preserves all rewarded units, ensuring a non-decreasing score. □

Interpretation SELECT- BEST and MERGED satisfy the *non-penalization principle*: adding more human references can only improve or maintain the score. □

Property B.3 (Limitation of averaging) For SIMPLE- AVERAGE,

$$\mathcal{F}_{\text{SIMPLE- AVG}}(\mathcal{R}_{n+1}) = \frac{n}{n+1}\mathcal{F}_{\text{SIMPLE- AVG}}(\mathcal{R}_n) + \frac{1}{n+1}f_{n+1}$$

Hence,

$$\mathcal{F}_{\text{SIMPLE- AVG}}(\mathcal{R}_{n+1}) \geq \mathcal{F}_{\text{SIMPLE- AVG}}(\mathcal{R}_n)$$

if and only if $f_{n+1} \geq \mathcal{F}_{\text{SIMPLE- AVG}}(\mathcal{R}_n)$. □

Proof sketch This follows from the recursive definition of the arithmetic mean: the average increases only if the new score exceeds the current mean. □

Interpretation Simple averaging fails to guarantee monotonicity: adding a valid but divergent reference may lower the overall score, revealing a trade-off between fairness and robustness to variation.

□

Property B.4 (Weighted averaging bounds and sensitivity) With softmax weights $w_i = \exp(\tau \cdot f_i)/\sum_j \exp(\tau \cdot f_j)$ for $\tau > 0$,

$$\min_i f_i \leq \sum_i w_i f_i \leq \max_i f_i,$$

and $\partial \mathcal{F}_{\text{WEIGHTED-AVG}}/\partial f_k \geq 0$ for each k. Adding a low-scoring reference can slightly decrease the total score if it receives nonzero weight.

Proof sketch A softmax-weighted sum is a convex combination. Gradients with respect to each f_k are nonnegative, but low-scoring references redistribute probability mass, which can lower the overall average. □

Interpretation Weighted averaging models graded human acceptability while maintaining boundedness. It captures how human evaluators tend to reward prototypical variants more strongly than rare alternatives. □

Property B.5 (Non-penalization principle) Among all strategies, SELECT- BEST and MERGED satisfy non-penalization strictly, while average-based strategies do not.

Interpretation This property summarizes the behavioral spectrum of multi-reference evaluation: SELECT- BEST corresponds to strict grading, MERGED reflects inclusive evaluation, and averaging-based strategies mediate graded fairness between these extremes. □

B.5 Conclusion

This chapter has outlined a general mathematical framework for multi-reference evaluation, independent of any specific metric or task. By treating evaluation as an aggregation problem over sets of valid linguistic variants, the framework provides a principled alternative to single-reference scoring and highlights the importance of representing linguistic diversity in evaluation design.

Although the formal development presented here is self-contained, its full integration into practical NLP evaluation–particularly within end-to-end, alignment-aware systems—remains a direction for future work. The JP-framework introduced throughout this book focuses on restoring comparability through alignment at the level of sentences, words, and structures. A complementary multi-reference layer would extend this principle further, allowing evaluation to reflect not only correspondence between system and reference representations, but also the multiplicity of valid human realizations.

In real-world applications, where models generate diverse outputs and operate across languages with heterogeneous segmentation and structural conventions, such a multi-reference extension would help ensure that alignment-based evaluation remains fair, robust, and sensitive to legitimate variation. Moreover, combining alignment with principled aggregation offers a path toward evaluation methods capable of handling both structural mismatches and representational diversity—two challenges that increasingly define modern end-to-end NLP.

Thus, while the present chapter establishes the theoretical foundations of multi-reference aggregation, its practical incorporation into alignment-based evaluation can be pursued as a natural continuation of this work. Developing such hybrid evaluation strategies represents an important avenue for future research, one that promises to strengthen the applicability and interpretability of evaluation by alignment in complex, real-world settings.

Glossary

accuracy The proportion of correctly predicted items among all evaluated items. In tagging tasks, this is typically computed over tokens; in structure prediction, it is less informative than overlap-based metrics.

alignment A mapping between elements in two sequences. In this chapter it refers to correspondence between system and gold sentences or tokens, including one-to-one, one-to-many, or many-to-many mappings.

alignment-based evaluation An evaluation method that compares system outputs and gold references by aligning segments at the sentence and token levels, allowing structural mismatches and partial matches. Inspired by sentence and word alignment in machine translation, it yields more nuanced and linguistically informed scores than exact string matching.

`aligning trees` A structural alignment framework for constituency tree comparison that identifies overlapping subtrees based on shared terminal yields. It aligns syntactic structures across treebanks with differing tagsets or annotation depths and reports coverage statistics that quantify the proportion of structurally aligned subtrees.

component-based evaluation A traditional practice of scoring individual pipeline modules (tokenization, tagging, parsing) separately, assuming consistent preprocessing.

edit distance A family of string-similarity metrics that count the minimum operations (insertions, deletions, substitutions) needed to transform one string into another. Levenshtein distance is the most common variant. In tokenization evaluation, it quantifies divergence between system and gold segmentations.

edit similarity A normalized similarity score derived from edit distance that quantifies how alike two strings are after removing whitespace.

end-to-end systems Models that map raw inputs directly to outputs without modular preprocessing stages. Their outputs may be incomparable under exact-match metrics unless alignment-aware evaluation is used.

J. Park, *Evaluation by Alignment*, Synthesis Lectures on Computer Science,
https://doi.org/10.1007/978-3-032-16563-3

errant A grammatical error correction evaluation toolkit that extracts edits and reports precision, recall, and $F_{0.5}$.

errant_compare The primary scorer in the `errant` framework. It aligns system edits with gold edits from M2 annotations, classifies them by operation type (Missing, Replacement, Unnecessary), and computes precision-, recall-, and $F_{0.5}$-oriented scores, including per-error-type breakdowns and multi-reference best-match evaluation.

exact match A matching criterion that requires predicted and gold spans to have identical start and end offsets (and, when applicable, identical labels).

false negative (FN) A relevant item (e.g., a true sentence boundary or token) that was not retrieved by the system. High FN typically indicates under-segmentation or boundary omission.

false positive (FP) An item identified by the system that does not match any item in the gold standard. In preprocessing, FP often corresponds to over-segmentation or spurious boundaries.

F_1 -score The harmonic mean of precision and recall. It balances under- and over-prediction by rewarding systems that perform well on both.

GLEU A fluency-oriented metric for grammatical error correction that scores a system by rewarding n-grams that appear in the reference correction but not in the source, and penalizing n-grams from the source that should have been changed but were left untouched. Unlike BLEU, which only measures overlap with the reference, GLEU also conditions on the source sentence and is explicitly sensitive to whether the system fixed what needed fixing without rewriting correct content.

gold standard A reference dataset with manually verified annotations considered correct for evaluation. In this chapter, gold tokenization and sentence boundaries are used as targets for alignment and scoring.

HOO A shared-task evaluation for grammatical error correction in which systems submit explicit edit proposals with character offsets, error types, and corrections. HOO is evaluated using F_1 over matched edits, rewarding exact agreement with reference corrections at the span and string level.

I-measure A token-level grammatical error correction metric that aligns the source, system output, and reference using three-way dynamic programming. It reports weighted accuracy and an improvement score I, quantifying how much a system improves (or degrades) the input relative to leaving it unedited.

jp-algorithm The jointly preprocessed alignment algorithm that realigns sentences and words across system and reference texts prior to task-specific scoring.

length distance A normalized measure of the difference in character lengths between two space-removed strings used as a proxy for sentence similarity.

mismatch A discrepancy between system and gold token or sentence boundaries. Causes include segmentation heuristics, normalization routines, or language-specific rules; mismatches affect both evaluation and downstream performance.

morphological segmentation The decomposition of orthographic words into morphemes (e.g., stems, affixes). Critical for agglutinative languages and a frequent source of tokenization mismatch.

n-gram A contiguous sequence of *n* tokens used in overlap-based evaluation metrics (e.g., BLEU, ROUGE, GLEU). Sensitive to surface differences in tokenization and phrasing.

normalization A preprocessing step that canonically rewrites surface forms (e.g., case-folding, Unicode normalization, apostrophe unification). Normalization may alter token boundaries and thus affect evaluation.

PARSEVAL/`EVALB` The standard constituency parsing evaluation protocol/tool that reports precision, recall, and F_1-score over bracket spans. Sensitive to token and sentence segmentation.

partial match A matching criterion that gives credit to overlapping spans that do not fully coincide. Sometimes used in semantic role labeling or information extraction.

precision The proportion of retrieved items (e.g., tokens or sentence boundaries) that are correct. High precision indicates few false positives and is especially relevant in over-segmentation-prone settings.

recall An evaluation metric measuring the proportion of relevant items (e.g., gold tokens or sentence boundaries) that were successfully retrieved by the system. Low recall indicates under-segmentation or missed boundaries.

`reference-less` evaluation An evaluation paradigm that scores grammatical error correction output without requiring a gold reference. It does not match system edits to human edits, but instead estimates grammaticality and fluency directly (e.g., via grammar checkers, feature-based models, or large language models acting as post-editors) and may combine this with a measure of adequacy to judge whether the system preserved the original meaning.

sentence alignment The process of pairing and, when necessary, merging or splitting sentences from two texts so that each aligned pair corresponds in content after removing whitespace.

subword unit A learned unit (e.g., BPE, unigram LM) that lies between characters and words. Subword-based systems complicate comparisons with word-based gold standards.

`tedeval` An evaluation toolkit for syntactic parsing based on *tree edit distance* (TED), which measures the minimal number of edit operations required to transform a predicted tree into a gold-standard tree. Unlike span-based metrics such as `EVALB`, it compares hierarchical structure rather than exact token alignment, allowing graded evaluation even when tokenization or segmentation differ.

true positive (TP) A correctly identified item—token or sentence boundary—that matches the gold standard. High TP indicates accurate predictions and is necessary for strong precision and recall.

UAS/LAS Unlabeled and labeled attachment scores for dependency parsing. UAS measures correct head selection regardless of label; LAS additionally requires a correct dependency label.

word alignment The process of aligning word sequences within already aligned sentence pairs, accommodating over- or under-segmentation by grouping tokens.

References

Abeillé, A. (Ed.). (2003). *Treebanks: Building and using parsed corpora*. Springer. ISBN: 978-1-4020-1334-8. https://doi.org/10.1007/978-94-010-0201-1

Alam, T., Khan, A., Alam, F. (2020). Punctuation restoration using transformer models for high- and low-resource languages. In W. Xu, A. Ritter, T. Baldwin, & A. Rahimi (Eds.), *Proceedings of the Sixth Workshop on Noisy User-Generated Text (W-NUT 2020)* (pp. 132–142) (Online November 2020). Association for Computational Linguistics. https://doi.org/10.18653/v1/2020.wnut-1.18

Belkebir, R., & Habash, N. (2021). Automatic error type annotation for Arabic. In A. Bisazza, & O. Abend (Eds.), *Proceedings of the 25th Conference on Computational Natural Language Learning* (pp. 596–606) (Online November 2021). Association for Computational Linguistics. https://doi.org/10.18653/v1/2021.conll-1.47

Bird, S., Klein, E., & Loper, E. (2009). *Natural Language processing with Python*. O'Reilly Media. http://shop.oreilly.com/product/9780596516499.do

Black, E., Abney, S. P., Flickinger, D., Gdaniec, C., Grishman, R., Harrison, P., Hindle, D., Ingria, R., Jelinek, F., Klavans, J., Liberman, M., Marcus, M., Roukos, S., Santorini, B., & Strzalkowski, T. (1991). A procedure for quantitatively comparing the syntactic coverage of English grammars. In *Proceedings of a Workshop on Speech and Natural Language* (pp. 306–311). Morgan Kaufmann.

Boyd, A. (2018). Using Wikipedia edits in low resource grammatical error correction. In W. Xu, A. Ritter, T. Baldwin, & A. Rahimi (Eds.), *Proceedings of the 2018 EMNLP Workshop W-NUT: The 4th Workshop on Noisy User-Generated Text*, Brussels, Belgium, November 2018 (pp. 79–84). Association for Computational Linguistics. https://doi.org/10.18653/v1/W18-6111

Bryant, C., Felice, M., Briscoe, T. (2017). Automatic annotation and evaluation of error types for grammatical error correction. In R. Barzilay, & M.-Y. Kan (Eds.), *Proceedings of the 55th Annual Meeting of the Association for Computational Linguistics (Volume 1: Long Papers)*, Vancouver, Canada, July 2017 (pp. 793–805). Association for Computational Linguistics. https://doi.org/10.18653/v1/P17-1074

Bryant, C., Felice, M., Andersen, Ø. E., & Briscoe, T. (2019). The BEA-2019 shared task on grammatical error correction. In *Proceedings of the Fourteenth Workshop on Innovative Use of NLP for Building Educational Applications*, Florence, Italy, August 2019 (pp. 52–75). Association for Computational Linguistics. https://doi.org/10.18653/v1/W19-4406

J. Park, *Evaluation by Alignment*, Synthesis Lectures on Computer Science,
https://doi.org/10.1007/978-3-032-16563-3

Bryant, C., Yuan, Z., Qorib, M. R., Cao, H., Ng, H. T., & Briscoe, T. (2023). Grammatical error correction: A survey of the state of the art. *Computational Linguistics, 49*(3), 643–701. https://doi.org/10.1162/coli_a_00478

Bryant, C. J. (2019). *Automatic annotation of error types for grammatical error correction*. PhD thesis, University of Cambridge, Churchill College, Cambridge, UK. https://doi.org/10.17863/CAM.40832

Calder, J. (1997). On aligning trees. In *Second Conference on Empirical Methods in Natural Language Processing* (pp. 75–80). https://aclanthology.org/W97-0308

Chomsky, N. (1957). *Syntactic structures*. Mouton & Co. ISBN: 9780262030908.

Chomsky, N. (1965). *Aspects of the theory of syntax*. The MIT Press. ISBN: 9780262030113. https://mitpress.mit.edu/books/aspects-theory-syntax

Cocke, J. (1969). *Programming languages and their compilers: Preliminary notes*. New York University. ISBN: B0007F4UOA.

Collins, M. (1999). *Head-driven statistical models for natural language parsing*. PhD thesis, University of Pennsylvania. http://www.cs.columbia.edu/~mcollins/papers/thesis.ps

Dahlmeier, D., & Ng, H. T. (2012). Better evaluation for grammatical error correction. In E. Fosler-Lussier, E. Riloff, & S. Bangalore (Eds.), *Proceedings of the 2012 Conference of the North American Chapter of the Association for Computational Linguistics: Human Language Technologies*, Montréal, Canada, June 2012 (pp. 568–572). Association for Computational Linguistics. https://aclanthology.org/N12-1067

Dale, R., & Kilgarriff, A. (2011). Helping our own: The HOO 2011 pilot shared task. In C. Gardent, & K. Striegnitz (Eds.), *Proceedings of the 13th European Workshop on Natural Language Generation*, Nancy, France, September 2011 (pp. 242–249). Association for Computational Linguistics. https://aclanthology.org/W11-2838/

Dozat, T., & Manning, C. D. (2017). Deep biaffine attention for neural dependency parsing. In *Proceedings of the 5th International Conference on Learning Representations (ICLR 2017)*, Toulon, France, November 2017. The International Conference on Learning Representations (ICLR). http://arxiv.org/abs/1611.01734

Dridan, R., & Oepen, S. (2012). Tokenization: Returning to a long solved problem—a survey, contrastive experiment, recommendations, and toolkit. In *Proceedings of the 50th Annual Meeting of the Association for Computational Linguistics (Volume 2: Short Papers)*, Jeju Island, Korea, 2012 (pp. 378–382). Association for Computational Linguistics. http://www.aclweb.org/anthology/P12-2074

Dyer, C., Kuncoro, A., Ballesteros, M., & Smith, N. A. (2016). Recurrent neural network grammars. In K. Knight, A. Nenkova, & O. Rambow (Eds.), *Proceedings of the 2016 Conference of the North American Chapter of the Association for Computational Linguistics: Human Language Technologies*, San Diego, CA, June 2016 (pp. 199–209). Association for Computational Linguistics. https://doi.org/10.18653/v1/N16-1024

Evang, K., Basile, V., Chrupała, G., & Bos, J. (2013). Elephant: Sequence labeling for word and sentence segmentation. In *Proceedings of the 2013 Conference on Empirical Methods in Natural Language Processing*, Seattle, Washington, USA, October 2013 (pp. 1422–1426). Association for Computational Linguistics. http://www.aclweb.org/anthology/D13-1146

Felice, M., & Briscoe, T. (2015). Towards a standard evaluation method for grammatical error detection and correction. In R. Mihalcea, J. Chai, & A. Sarkar (Eds.), *Proceedings of the 2015 Conference of the North American Chapter of the Association for Computational Linguistics: Human Language Technologies*, Denver, Colorado, 2015 (pp. 578–587). Association for Computational Linguistics. https://aclanthology.org/N15-1060/

Fernández-González, D., & Gómez-Rodríguez, C. (2019). Faster shift-reduce constituent parsing with a non-binary, bottom-up strategy. *Artificial Intelligence, 275*, 559–574. ISSN: 0004-3702. https://doi.org/10.1016/j.artint.2019.07.006

Fernández-González, D., & Gómez-Rodríguez, C. (2020). Enriched in-order linearization for faster sequence-to-sequence constituent parsing. In *Proceedings of the 58th Annual Meeting of the Association for Computational Linguistics*, Online, July 2020 (pp. 4092–4099). Association for Computational Linguistics. https://doi.org/10.18653/v1/2020.acl-main.376

Fu, X.-Y., Chen, C., Laskar, M. T. R., Bhushan, S., & Corston-Oliver, S. (2021). Improving punctuation restoration for speech transcripts via external data. In W. Xu, A. Ritter, T. Baldwin, & A. Rahimi (Eds.), *Proceedings of the Seventh Workshop on Noisy User-Generated Text (W-NUT 2021)* (pp. 168–174) (Online November 2021). Association for Computational Linguistics. https://doi.org/10.18653/v1/2021.wnut-1.19

Gale, W. A., & Church, K. W. (1993). A program for aligning sentences in bilingual corpora. *Computational Linguistics, 19*(1), 75–102. https://aclanthology.org/J93-1004

Gillick, D. (2009). Sentence boundary detection and the problem with the U.S. In *Proceedings of Human Language Technologies: The 2009 Annual Conference of the North American Chapter of the Association for Computational Linguistics, Companion Volume: Short Papers*, Boulder, Colorado, 2009 (pp. 241–244). Association for Computational Linguistics. http://www.aclweb.org/anthology/N/N09/N09-2061

González-Gallardo, C.-E., & Torres-Moreno, J.-M. (2018). WiSeBE: Window-based sentence boundary evaluation. In *Advances in Computational Intelligence: Proceedings of the17th Mexican International Conference on Artificial Intelligence (Part II), MICAI 2018*, Guadalajara, Mexico, October 2018 (pp. 119–131). Springer. https://doi.org/10.1007/978-3-030-04497-8

Grabisch, M., Marichal, J.-L., Mesiar, R., & Pap, E. (2009). *Aggregation functions*. Encyclopedia of mathematics and its applications. Cambridge University Press.

Gu, Y., Huang, Z., Zeng, M., Qiu, M., & Park, J. (2025). Improving automatic grammatical error annotation for Chinese through linguistically-informed error typology. In O. Rambow, L. Wanner, M. Apidianaki, H. Al-Khalifa, B. Di Eugenio, & S. Schockaert (Eds.), *Proceedings of the 31st International Conference on Computational Linguistics*, Abu Dhabi, UAE, January 2025 (pp. 2781–2798). Association for Computational Linguistics. https://aclanthology.org/2025.coling-main.189/

Hinson, C., Huang, H.-H., Chen, H.-H. (2020). Heterogeneous recycle generation for Chinese grammatical error correction. In D. Scott, N. Bel, & C. Zong (Eds.), *Proceedings of the 28th International Conference on Computational Linguistics*, Barcelona, Spain (pp. 2191–2201) (Online), December 2020. International Committee on Computational Linguistics. https://doi.org/10.18653/v1/2020.coling-main.199

Jo, E. L., Park, A. Y., & Park, J. (2024). A novel alignment-based approach for PARSEVAL measures. *Computational Linguistics, 50*(3), 1181–1190. https://doi.org/10.1162/coli_a_00512

Jo, E. L., Park, A. Y., Zhang, G. T., Wang, I. X., Wang, J., Mao, M., & Park, J. (2024b). An untold story of preprocessing task evaluation: An alignment-based joint evaluation approach. In N. Calzolari, M.-Y. Kan, V. Hoste, A. Lenci, S. Sakti, & N. Xue (Eds.), *Proceedings of the 2024 Joint International Conference on Computational Linguistics, Language Resources and Evaluation (LREC-COLING 2024)*, Torino, Italy, May 2024 (pp. 1327–1338). ELRA and ICCL. https://aclanthology.org/2024.lrec-main.119

Kaplan, R. M. (2005). A method for tokenizing text. In A. Arppe, L. Carlson, K. Lindén, J. Piitulainen, M. Suominen, M. Vainio, H. Westerlund, & A. Yli-Jyrä (Eds.), *Inquiries into Words, Constraints and Contexts-Festschrift for Kimmo Koskenniemi on his 60th Birthday* (chap. 6, pp. 55–64). CSLI Publications, Stanford, CA, 2005. ISBN: 1557-5772.

Kasai, J., Frank, B., McCoy, T., Rambow, O., & Nasr, A. (2017). TAG parsing with neural networks and vector representations of supertags. In *Proceedings of the 2017 Conference on Empirical*

Methods in Natural Language Processing, Copenhagen, Denmark, September 2017 (pp. 1712–1722). Association for Computational Linguistics. https://doi.org/10.18653/v1/D17-1180

Kasai, J., Frank, R., Xu, P., Merrill, W., & Rambow, O. (2018). End-to-end graph-based TAG parsing with neural networks. In *Proceedings of the 2018 Conference of the North American Chapter of the Association for Computational Linguistics: Human Language Technologies, Volume 1 (Long Papers)*, New Orleans, Louisiana, June 2018 (pp. 1181–1194). Association for Computational Linguistics. https://doi.org/10.18653/v1/N18-1107

Kasami, T. (1966). *An efficient recognition and syntax-analysis algorithm for context-free languages*. Technical report, University of Illinois at Urbana-Champaign. http://hdl.handle.net/2142/74304

Kim, M., & Park, J. (2022). A note on constituent parsing for Korean. *Natural Language Engineering, 28*(2), 199–222. https://doi.org/10.1017/S1351324920000479

Kitaev, N., & Klein, D. (2018). Constituency parsing with a self-attentive encoder. In *Proceedings of the 56th Annual Meeting of the Association for Computational Linguistics (Volume 1: Long Papers)*, Melbourne, Australia, July 2018 (pp. 2675–2685). Association for Computational Linguistics. http://aclweb.org/anthology/P18-1249

Kitaev, N., Cao, S., & Klein, D. (2019). Multilingual constituency parsing with self-attention and pre-training. In *Proceedings of the 57th Annual Meeting of the Association for Computational Linguistics*, Florence, Italy, July 2019 (pp. 3499–3505). Association for Computational Linguistics. https://www.aclweb.org/anthology/P19-1340

Koehn, P. (2005). Europarl: A parallel corpus for statistical machine translation. In *Proceedings of the Tenth Machine Translation Summit X*, Phuket, Thailand, 2005 (pp. 79–86). International Association for Machine Translation.

Koehn, P., Hoang, H., Birch, A., Callison-Burch, C., Federico, M., Bertoldi, N., Cowan, B., Shen, W., Moran, C., Zens, R., Dyer, C., Bojar, O., Constantin, A., & Herbst, E. (2007). Moses: Open source toolkit for statistical machine translation. In *Proceedings of the 45th Annual Meeting of the Association for Computational Linguistics Companion Volume Proceedings of the Demo and Poster Sessions*, Prague, Czech Republic, 2007 (pp. 177–180). Association for Computational Linguistics. http://www.aclweb.org/anthology/P07-2045

Korre, K., Chatzipanagiotou, M., & Pavlopoulos, J. (2021). ELERRANT: Automatic grammatical error type classification for Greek. In R. Mitkov, & G. Angelova (Eds.), *Proceedings of the International Conference on Recent Advances in Natural Language Processing (RANLP 2021)*, Held Online, September 2021 (pp. 708–717). INCOMA Ltd. https://aclanthology.org/2021.ranlp-1.81/

Lee, K., Lewis, M., & Zettlemoyer, L. (2016). Global neural CCG parsing with optimality guarantees. In *Proceedings of the 2016 Conference on Empirical Methods in Natural Language Processing*, Austin, Texas, November 2016 (pp. 2366–2376). Association for Computational Linguistics. https://aclweb.org/anthology/D16-1262

Lewis, M., Lee, K., & Zettlemoyer, L. (2016). LSTM CCG parsing. In *Proceedings of the 2016 Conference of the North American Chapter of the Association for Computational Linguistics: Human Language Technologies*, San Diego, California, June 2016 (pp. 221–231). Association for Computational Linguistics. http://www.aclweb.org/anthology/N16-1026

Lim, K., & Park, J. (2024). Real-world sentence boundary detection using multi-task learning: A case study on French. *Natural Language Engineering, 30*(1), 150–170. https://doi.org/10.1017/S1351324922000134

Lin, C.-Y. (2004). ROUGE: A package for automatic evaluation of summaries. In *Text Summarization Branches Out*, Barcelona, Spain, July 2004 (pp. 74–81). Association for Computational Linguistics. https://aclanthology.org/W04-1013/

Liu, J., & Zhang, Y. (2017). In-order transition-based constituent parsing. *Transactions of the Association for Computational Linguistics, 5*, 413–424. https://doi.org/10.1162/tacl_a_00070

Loper, E., & Bird, S. (2002). NLTK: The natural language toolkit. In *Proceedings of the ACL-02 Workshop on Effective Tools and Methodologies for Teaching Natural Language Processing and Computational Linguistics*, Philadelphia, Pennsylvania, USA, July 2002 (pp. 63–70). Association for Computational Linguistics. https://doi.org/10.3115/1118108.1118117

Manning, C., Surdeanu, M., Bauer, J., Finkel, J., Bethard, S., & McClosky, D. (2014). The Stanford CoreNLP natural language processing toolkit. In K. Bontcheva, & J. Zhu (Eds.), *Proceedings of 52nd Annual Meeting of the Association for Computational Linguistics: System Demonstrations*, Baltimore, Maryland, June 2014 (pp. 55–60). Association for Computational Linguistics. https://doi.org/10.3115/v1/P14-5010

Marcus, M. P., Marcinkiewicz, M. A., & Santorini, B. (1993). Building a large annotated corpus of English: The Penn Treebank. *Computational linguistics, 19*(2), 313–330. https://aclanthology.org/J93-2004

Masciolini, A., Caines, A., De Clercq, O., Kruijsbergen, J., Kurfalı, M., Muñoz Sánchez, R., Volodina, E., & Östling, R. (2025a). The MultiGEC-2025 shared task on multilingual grammatical error correction at NLP4CALL. In R. Muñoz Sánchez, D. Alfter, E. Volodina, & J. Kallas (Eds.), *Proceedings of the 14th Workshop on Natural Language Processing for Computer Assisted Language Learning*, Tallinn, Estonia, March 2025 (pp. 1–33). University of Tartu Library. ISBN: 978-9908-53-112-0. https://aclanthology.org/2025.nlp4call-1.1/

Masciolini, A., Caines, A., De Clercq, O., Kruijsbergen, J., Kurfalı, M., Muñoz Sánchez, R., Volodina, E., Östling, R., Allkivi, K., Arhar Holdt, Š., Auzina, I., Darģis, R., Drakonaki, E., Frey, J.-C., Glišić, I., Kikilintza, P., Nicolas, L., Romanyshyn, M., Rosen, A., Rozovskaya, A., Suluste, K., Syvokon, O., Tantos, A., Touriki, D.-O., Tsiotskas, K., Tsourilla, E., Varsamopoulos, V., Wisniewski, K., Žagar, A., & Zesch, T. (2025b). Towards better language representation in Natural Language Processing. *International Journal of Learner Corpus Research*. ISSN: 2215-1478. https://doi.org/10.1075/ijlcr.24033.mas

McDonald, R., Nivre, J., Quirmbach-Brundage, Y., Goldberg, Y., Das, D., Ganchev, K., Hall, K., Petrov, S., Zhang, H., Täckström, O., Bedini, C., Bertomeu Castelló, N., & Lee, J. (2013). Universal dependency annotation for multilingual parsing. In H. Schuetze, P. Fung, & M. Poesio (Eds.), *Proceedings of the 51st Annual Meeting of the Association for Computational Linguistics (Volume 2: Short Papers)*, Sofia, Bulgaria, August 2013 (pp. 92–97). Association for Computational Linguistics. https://aclanthology.org/P13-2017

Náplava, J., Straka, M., Straková, J., & Rosen, A. (2022). Czech grammar error correction with a large and diverse corpus. *Transactions of the Association for Computational Linguistics, 10*, 452–467. https://doi.org/10.1162/tacl_a_00470

Napoles, C., Sakaguchi, K., Post, M., & Tetreault, J. (2015). Ground truth for grammatical error correction metrics. In C. Zong, & M. Strube (Eds.), *Proceedings of the 53rd Annual Meeting of the Association for Computational Linguistics and the 7th International Joint Conference on Natural Language Processing (Volume 2: Short Papers)*, Beijing, China, July 2015 (pp. 588–593). Association for Computational Linguistics. https://doi.org/10.3115/v1/P15-2097

Napoles, C., Sakaguchi, K., Post, M., & Tetreault, J. (2016a). *GLEU without tuning*. https://arxiv.org/abs/1605.02592

Napoles, C., Sakaguchi, K., Tetreault, J. (2016b). There's no comparison: Reference-less evaluation metrics in grammatical error correction. In J. Su, K. Duh, & X. Carreras (Eds.), *Proceedings of the 2016 Conference on Empirical Methods in Natural Language Processing*, Austin, Texas, November 2016 (pp. 2109–2115). Association for Computational Linguistics. https://doi.org/10.18653/v1/D16-1228

Nivre, J., De Marneffe, M.C., Ginter, F., Goldberg, Y., Hajic, J., Manning, C.D., McDonald, R., Petrov, S., Pyysalo, S., Silveira, N., Tsarfaty, R., & Zeman, D. (2016). Universal dependencies v1: A multilingual treebank collection. In L. von Ahn (Ed.), *Proceedings of the Tenth Interna-*

tional Conference on Language Resources and Evaluation (LREC 2016), Portorož, Slovenia, 2016 (pp. 1659–1666). European Language Resources Association (ELRA). https://www.aclweb.org/anthology/L16-1262

Nivre, J., de Marneffe, M.-C., Ginter, F., Hajič, J., Manning, C. D., Pyysalo, S., Schuster, S., Tyers, F., & Zeman, D. (2020). Universal dependencies v2: An evergrowing multilingual treebank collection. In *Proceedings of the 12th Language Resources and Evaluation Conference*, Marseille, France, May 2020 (pp. 4034–4043). European Language Resources Association. ISBN: 979-10-95546-34-4. https://www.aclweb.org/anthology/2020.lrec-1.497

Omelianchuk, K., Atrasevych, V., Chernodub, A., Skurzhanskyi, O. (2020). GECToR—Grammatical error correction: Tag, not rewrite. In *Proceedings of the Fifteenth Workshop on Innovative Use of NLP for Building Educational Applications*, Seattle, WA, USA → Online, July 2020 (pp. 163–170). Association for Computational Linguistics. https://doi.org/10.18653/v1/2020.bea-1.16

Östling, R., Kurfali, M., & Caines, A. (2025). LLM-based post-editing as reference-free GEC evaluation. In E. Kochmar, B. Alhafni, M. Bexte, J. Burstein, A. Horbach, R. Laarmann-Quante, A. Tack, V. Yaneva, & Z. Yuan (Eds.), *Proceedings of the 20th Workshop on Innovative Use of NLP for Building Educational Applications (BEA 2025)*, Vienna, Austria, July 2025 (pp. 213–224). Association for Computational Linguistics. ISBN: 979-8-89176-270-1. https://aclanthology.org/2025.bea-1.16/

Palmer, D. D., & Hearst, M. A. (1997). Adaptive multilingual sentence boundary disambiguation. *Computational Linguistics, 23*(2), 241–267. ISSN: 0891-2017. http://aclweb.org/anthology/J/J06/J06-4003.pdf

Papineni, K., Roukos, S., Ward, T., & Zhu, W.-J. (2002). BLEU: A method for automatic evaluation of machine translation. In Isabelle, P., Charniak, E., & D. Lin (Eds.), *Proceedings of the 40th Annual Meeting of the Association for Computational Linguistics*, Philadelphia, Pennsylvania, USA, July 2002 (pp. 311–318). Association for Computational Linguistics. https://doi.org/10.3115/1073083.1073135

Park, J., & Tyers, F. (2019). A new annotation scheme for the sejong part-of-speech tagged corpus. In *Proceedings of the 13th Linguistic Annotation Workshop*, Florence, Italy, August 2019. Association for Computational Linguistics (pp. 195–202). https://www.aclweb.org/anthology/W19-4022

Park, J., Hong, J.-P., & Cha, J.-W. (2016). Korean language resources for everyone. In *Proceedings of the 30th Pacific Asia Conference on Language, Information and Computation: Oral Papers (PACLIC 30)*, Seoul, Korea, 2016 (pp. 49–58). http://aclweb.org/anthology/Y/Y16/Y16-2002.pdf

Park, J., Wang, J., Jo, E. L., & Park, A. Y. (2024). jp-evalb: Robust alignment-based PARSEVAL measures. In K.-W. Chang, A. Lee, & N. Rajani (Eds.), *Proceedings of the 2024 Conference of the North American Chapter of the Association for Computational Linguistics: Human Language Technologies (Volume 3: System Demonstrations)*, Mexico City, Mexico, June 2024 (pp. 70–77). Association for Computational Linguistics. https://aclanthology.org/2024.naacl-demo.7

Petrov, S., & Klein, D. (2007). Improved inference for unlexicalized parsing. In *Human Language Technologies 2007: The Conference of the North American Chapter of the Association for Computational Linguistics; Proceedings of the Main Conference*, Rochester, New York, 2007 (pp. 404–411). Association for Computational Linguistics. http://www.aclweb.org/anthology/N/N07/N07-1051

Petrov, S., Das, D., & McDonald, R. (2012). A universal part-of-speech tagset. In *Proceedings of the Eighth International Conference on Language Resources and Evaluation (LREC-2012)* (pp. 2089–2096), Istanbul, Turkey, 2012. European Language Resources Association (ELRA). ISBN 978-2-9517408-7-7.

Poláček, M., Červa, P., Žďánský, J., & Weingartová, L. (2023). Online punctuation restoration using ELECTRA model for streaming ASR systems. In *Proceedings of INTERSPEECH 2023*, Dublin, Ireland, 2023 (pp. 446–450). International Speech Communication Association. https://doi.org/10.21437/Interspeech.2023-664

Qi, P., Zhang, Y., Zhang, Y., Bolton, J., Manning, C. D. (2020). Stanza: A Python natural language processing toolkit for many human languages. In A. Celikyilmaz, & T.-H. Wen (Eds.), *Proceedings of the 58th Annual Meeting of the Association for Computational Linguistics: System Demonstrations*, Online, July 2020 (pp. 101–108). Association for Computational Linguistics. https://doi.org/10.18653/v1/2020.acl-demos.14

Qiu, M., Nguyen, T. M., Huang, Z., Li, Z., Gu, Y., Gao, Q., Liu, S., & Park, J. (2025). Multilingual grammatical error annotation: Combining language-agnostic framework with language-specific flexibility. In E. Kochmar, B. Alhafni, M. Bexte, J. Burstein, A. Horbach, R. Laarmann-Quante, A. Tack, V. Yaneva, & Z. Yuan (Eds.), *Proceedings of the 20th Workshop on Innovative Use of NLP for Building Educational Applications (BEA 2025)*, Vienna, Austria, July 2025 (pp. 202–212). Association for Computational Linguistics. ISBN: 979-8-89176-270-1. https://aclanthology.org/2025.bea-1.15/

Read, J., Dridan, R., Oepen, S., & Solberg, L. J. (2012). Sentence boundary detection: A long solved problem? In *Proceedings of COLING 2012: Posters*, Mumbai, India, 2012 (pp. 985–994). The COLING 2012 Organizing Committee. http://www.aclweb.org/anthology/C12-2096

Reynar, J. C., & Ratnaparkhi, A. (1997). A maximum entropy approach to identifying sentence boundaries. In *Proceedings of the Fifth Conference on Applied Natural Language Processing*, Washington, DC, USA, March 1997 (pp. 16–19). Association for Computational Linguistics. https://doi.org/10.3115/974557.974561

Roark, B., Harper, M.P., Charniak, E., Dorr, B.J., Johnson, M., Kahn, J.G., Liu, Y., Ostendorf, M., Hale, J., Krasnyanskaya, A., Lease, M., Shafran, I., Snover, M., Stewart, R., & Yung, L. (2006). SParseval: Evaluation metrics for parsing speech. In *Proceedings of the Fifth International Conference on Language Resources and Evaluation (LREC'06)*, Genoa, Italy, May 2006 (pp. 333–338). European Language Resources Association (ELRA). http://www.lrec-conf.org/proceedings/lrec2006/pdf/116_pdf.pdf

Rothe, S., Mallinson, J., Malmi, E., Krause, S., Severyn, A. (2021). A simple recipe for multilingual grammatical error correction. In *Proceedings of the 59th Annual Meeting of the Association for Computational Linguistics and the 11th International Joint Conference on Natural Language Processing (Volume 2: Short Papers)*, Online, August 2021 (pp. 702–707). Association for Computational Linguistics. https://doi.org/10.18653/v1/2021.acl-short.89

Sakaguchi, K., Napoles, C., Post, M., & Tetreault, J. (2016). Reassessing the goals of grammatical error correction: Fluency instead of grammaticality. *Transactions of the Association for Computational Linguistics, 4*, 169–182. https://doi.org/10.1162/tacl_a_00091

Seddah, D., Tsarfaty, R., Kübler, S., Candito, M., Choi, J.D., Farkas, R., Foster, J., Goenaga, I., Gojenola, K., Goldberg, Y., Green, S., Habash, N., Kuhlmann, M., Maier, W., Nivre, J., Przepiórkowski, A., Roth, R., Seeker, W., Versley, Y., Vincze, V., Woliński, M., Wróblewska, A., & de la Clergerie, E. V. (2013). Overview of the SPMRL 2013 shared task: A cross-framework evaluation of parsing morphologically rich languages. In *Proceedings of the Fourth Workshop on Statistical Parsing of Morphologically-Rich Languages*, Seattle, Washington, USA, October 2013 (pp. 146–182). Association for Computational Linguistics. http://www.aclweb.org/anthology/W13-4917

Seddah, D., Kübler, S., & Tsarfaty, R. (2014). Introducing the SPMRL 2014 shared task on parsing morphologically-rich languages. In *Proceedings of the First Joint Workshop on Statistical Parsing of Morphologically Rich Languages and Syntactic Analysis of Non-Canonical Languages*, Dublin, Ireland, August 2014 (pp. 103–109). Dublin City University. https://www.aclweb.org/anthology/W14-6111

Sonawane, A., Vishwakarma, S. K., Srivastava, B., & Singh, A. K. (2020). Generating inflectional errors for grammatical error correction in Hindi. In B. Shmueli, & Y. J. Huang (Eds.), *Proceedings of the 1st Conference of the Asia-Pacific Chapter of the Association for Computational Linguistics and the 10th International Joint Conference on Natural Language Processing: Student Research Workshop*, Suzhou, China, December 2020 (pp. 165–171). Association for Computational Linguistics. https://aclanthology.org/2020.aacl-srw.24

Stanojević, M., & Steedman, M. (2020). Max-margin incremental CCG parsing. In *Proceedings of the 58th Annual Meeting of the Association for Computational Linguistics*, Online, July 2020 (pp. 4111–4122). Association for Computational Linguistics. https://doi.org/10.18653/v1/2020.acl-main.378

Treviso, M., Shulby, C., & Aluísio, S. (2017). Evaluating word embeddings for sentence boundary detection in speech transcripts. In *Proceedings of the 11th Brazilian Symposium in Information and Human Language Technology*, Uberlândia, Brazil, October 2017 (pp. 151–160). Sociedade Brasileira de Computação. https://www.aclweb.org/anthology/W17-6618

Tsarfaty, R., Nivre, J., & Andersson, E. (2012). Joint evaluation of morphological segmentation and syntactic parsing. In *Proceedings of the 50th Annual Meeting of the Association for Computational Linguistics (Volume 2: Short Papers)*, Jeju Island, Korea, July 2012 (pp. 6–10). Association for Computational Linguistics. http://www.aclweb.org/anthology/P12-2002

Vinyals, O., Kaiser, L., Koo, T., Petrov, S., Sutskever, I., & Hinton, G. E. (2015). Grammar as a foreign language. In C. Cortes, N. D. Lawrence, D. D. Lee, M. Sugiyama, & R. Garnett (Eds.), *Advances in neural information processing systems* (Vol. 28, pp. 2773–2781). Curran Associates, Inc. http://papers.nips.cc/paper/5635-grammar-as-a-foreign-language.pdf

Wang, J., Qiu, M., Gu, Y., Huang, Z., & Park, J. (2025). Refined evaluation for end-to-end grammatical error correction using an alignment-based approach. In Rambow, O., Wanner, L., Apidianaki, M., Al-Khalifa, H., Di Eugenio, B., & Schockaert, S. (Eds.), *Proceedings of the 31st International Conference on Computational Linguistics*, Abu Dhabi, UAE, January 2025 (pp. 774–785). Association for Computational Linguistics. https://aclanthology.org/2025.coling-main.52/

Wei, Y., Wu, Y., Lan, M. (2020). A span-based linearization for constituent trees. In *Proceedings of the 58th Annual Meeting of the Association for Computational Linguistics*, Online, July 2020 (pp. 3267–3277). Association for Computational Linguistics. https://doi.org/10.18653/v1/2020.acl-main.299

Yamaki, R., Taniguchi, T., Mochihashi, D. (2023). Holographic CCG parsing. In *Proceedings of the 61st Annual Meeting of the Association for Computational Linguistics (Volume 1: Long Papers)*, Toronto, Canada, July 2023 (pp. 262–276). Association for Computational Linguistics. https://doi.org/10.18653/v1/2023.acl-long.15

Yannakoudakis, H., Andersen, Ø. E., Geranpayeh, A., Briscoe, T., & Nicholls, D. (2018). Developing an automated writing placement system for ESL learners. *Applied Measurement in Education, 31*(3), 251–267. ISSN: 0895-7347. https://doi.org/10.1080/08957347.2018.1464447

Yoon, S., Park, S., Kim, G., Cho, J., Park, K., Kim, G. T., Seo, M., & Oh, A. (2023). Towards standardizing Korean grammatical error correction: Datasets and annotation. In *Proceedings of the 61st Annual Meeting of the Association for Computational Linguistics (Volume 1: Long Papers)*, Toronto, Canada, July 2023 (pp. 6713–6742). Association for Computational Linguistics. https://aclanthology.org/2023.acl-long.371

Younger, D. H. (1967). Recognition and parsing of context-free languages in time n3. *Information and Control, 10*(2), 189–208. ISSN: 0019-9958. https://doi.org/10.1016/S0019-9958(67)80007-X

Yuan, W., Neubig, G., & Liu, P. (2021). BARTScore: Evaluating generated text as text generation. In M. Ranzato, A. Beygelzimer, Y. Dauphin, P. S. Liang, & J. Wortman Vaughan (Eds.), *Advances in Neural Information Processing Systems 34 (NeurIPS 2021)* (Vol. 34, pp. 27263–27277). Curran Associates, Inc. https://proceedings.neurips.cc/paper_files/paper/2021/file/e4d2b6e6fdeca3e60e0f1a62fee3d9dd-Paper.pdf

Zeman, D., Popel, M., Straka, M., Hajič, J., Nivre, J., Ginter, F., Luotolahti, J., Pyysalo, S., Petrov, S., Potthast, M., Tyers, F., Badmaeva, E., Gokirmak, M., Nedoluzhko, A., Cinková, S., Hajič Jr., J., Hlaváčová, J., Kettnerová, V., Urešová, Z., Kanerva, J., ... Li, J. (2017). CoNLL 2017 shared task: Multilingual parsing from raw text to universal dependencies. In *Proceedings of the CoNLL 2017 Shared Task: Multilingual Parsing from Raw Text to Universal Dependencies*, Vancouver, Canada, August 2017 (pp. 1–19). Association for Computational Linguistics. https://doi.org/10.18653/v1/K17-3001

Zeman, D., Hajic, J., Popel, M., Potthast, M., Straka, M., Ginter, F., Nivre, J., Petrov, S. (2018). CoNLL 2018 shared task: Multilingual parsing from raw text to universal dependencies. In D. Zeman, & J. Hajič (Eds.), *Proceedings of the CoNLL 2018 Shared Task: Multilingual Parsing from Raw Text to Universal Dependencies*, Brussels, Belgium, October 2018 (pp. 1–21). Association for Computational Linguistics. https://doi.org/10.18653/v1/K18-2001

Zeng, M., Kuang, J., Qiu, M., Song, J., & Park, J. (2024). Evaluating prompting strategies for grammatical error correction based on language proficiency. In N. Calzolari, M.-Y. Kan, V. Hoste, A. Lenci, S. Sakti, & N. Xue (Eds.), *Proceedings of the 2024 Joint International Conference on Computational Linguistics, Language Resources and Evaluation (LREC-COLING 2024)*, Torino, Italy, May 2024 (pp. 6426–6430). ELRA and ICCL. https://aclanthology.org/2024.lrec-main.569

Zhang, T., Kishore, V., Wu, F., Weinberger, K.Q., & Artzi, Y. (2019). BERTScore: Evaluating text generation with BERT. In *Proceedings of the 8th International Conference on Learning Representations 2020*. https://openreview.net/forum?id=SkeHuCVFDr

Zhang, Y., Li, Z., Bao, Z., Li, J., Zhang, B., Li, C., Huang, F., & Zhang, M. (2022). MuCGEC: A multi-reference multi-source evaluation dataset for Chinese grammatical error correction. In *Proceedings of the 2022 Conference of the North American Chapter of the Association for Computational Linguistics: Human Language Technologies*, Seattle, United States, July 2022 (pp. 3118–3130). Association for Computational Linguistics. https://doi.org/10.18653/v1/2022.naacl-main.227

Index

J. Park, *Evaluation by Alignment*, Synthesis Lectures on Computer Science,
https://doi.org/10.1007/978-3-032-16563-3

The manufacturer's authorised representative in the EU is Springer Nature Customer Service Centre GmbH, Europaplatz 3, 69115 Heidelberg, Germany. If you have any concerns regarding our products, please contact ProductSafety@springernature.com

Printed and bound by CPI Group (UK) Ltd, Croydon, CR0 4YY
17/09/2026
02218438-0011